**Battered Child, Broken Man** contains real life stories about Bill Ramsey and his prison experiences in the mid-1960s. It also contains real stories and testimonies from some Texas Death Row inmates and an anonymous youth on probation but spared from prison because of Bill's sharing with him. The gut-wrenching reality captivates and holds your attention. This is a must read for all persons heading down a poor-choice path to imprisonment!

Here is what others say about Ramsey's volunteer Chaplaincy:

"I have traveled the world and met many awesome men of God; Bill Ramsey is one such man . . . a true testimony to the power of our Lord."

-Joseph Franklin
Austin, TX

"We appreciate you and your ministry. It is a privilege to be part of such a great ministry team."

-Mike & DeAnne Barber
Barber Ministries
DeSoto, TX

"He has a heart for prisoners and wants to have the opportunity to share the gospel with as many as possible. I have witnessed his love for his Savior and enthusiasm to serve Christ."

-Dr. Richard Vaughan
Fletcher Emanuel Church Alive
Lumberton, TX

WIlliam and Denise Ramsey grev   ⁀ ⁀ East Texas
ministered in almost all prisons in T
have spent most of their lives in sou
ordinary people have a story to tell

BATTERED CHILD, BROKEN MAN

"Thrown in to Die and Lived to Tell Why!"

BILL RAMSEY

WESTBOW
PRESS
A DIVISION OF THOMAS NELSON

Parts first printed as **From A Distance—I Can See God** by the Kerusso Company, 1995. ISBN: 0-927760-15-0

WestBow Press books may be ordered through booksellers or by contacting:

WestBow Press
A Division of Thomas Nelson
1663 Liberty Drive
Bloomington, IN 47403
www.westbowpress.com
1-(866) 928-1240

ISBN: 978-1-4497-3835-8 (hc)
ISBN: 978-1-4497-3834-1 (sc)
ISBN: 978-1-4497-3833-4 (e)

Library of Congress Control Number: 2012901115

Printed in the United States of America

WestBow Press rev. date: 2/15/2012

Table of Contents

Dedication

I dedicate this book to . . .

➢ The Lord Jesus, my Lord and Savior.

➢ My loving wife Denise, who modeled for me the unconditional love of God the Father.

➢ All those who endured the horrendous suffering in "the Hole".

Especially those who died in "the Hole" and never lived to tell . . .

I am their voice.

Acknowledgements

I appreciate and wish to thank . . .

a) All those who joined with my wife and prayed for me.
b) Pastor Steve Hays who taught my wife about unconditional love. He not only married us, but he prayed with my wife when I would disappear and helped in so many ways I cannot count them.
c) All the ministers who prayed for and with me.
d) Pastor Tommy Burchfield who spoke a prophecy over me that I would never again be the same man. From that time on, I truly lived out that prophetic word.
e) All those who were wonderful Christian role models; this was a great source of strength for me.
f) All those who prayed for me and nurtured me in my Christian walk.
g) God. He is the only one who could change this broken man's life.
h) My wife Denise who showed me God's unconditional love through their lives of loving me until I could love myself and them, too. God bless them.
i) Dianne Haneke, PhD, who edited the grammar in this book.

j) Matthew Chance, my grandson who prepared this book for publishing.

These people gave me the encouragement I never received until I met God's people who know how to love unconditionally. I hope this book blesses many, but I wrote it to hopefully spare others from this tragedy and waste of life. Then I will know all I have experienced will have been worth it.

Foreword

"*From time to time the Good Lord raises up a simple, sincere, strong voice of an impassioned, Christian heart to bear witness to God's own children. Chaplain Bill Ramsey is such a voice. Bill reminds me of what Nathaniel might have been like when our Lord said of him "behold, a man in whom I find no guile."*

After seeing, hearing and reading this brother, I can highly recommend him to you and your church family. Invite Bill and his companion Denise, to visit and share their life message. Wow! What an exciting, true story they have to share with the Family of God. You and your people will love them and the Christ they serve even more after sharing in their witness.

Bill and Denise are servants of the Lord. They will complement and embrace any local, New Testament Church. They do not impose any agenda of their own but will work with the minister and the local church, regardless of its denominational affiliation. Bill and Denise will be your friend."

Sincerely, Pastor Bob Arnold
Church of God
Port Arthur, TX

"It is refreshing to witness the marvelous transformation of the grace of God in someone's life. It is equally refreshing to see that person yield their life to serve God. I praise the Lord for Bill Ramsey and I would like to give my whole-hearted recommendation to Bill and Denise as they seek to serve Christ. Bill is a yielded servant that God is using."

Sincerely, Dr. Steve Hays
Pastor Fellowship Baptist Church
Nederland, TX

Preface

In the beginning there was light. That was the vision, which came to me in the heavy silence of total darkness and the utter despair of four months' confinement in *"the Hole"*—a two-foot by two foot steel box designed for punishment. In that distant light, as if peering through the wrong end of a telescope, I witnessed the face of God.

This is the account of how I got there and how. After a lifetime of denying God, I came to realize God had a purpose for me in this mortal life—a purpose beyond my self-serving life of alcohol, drugs, and crime.

In the isolation of that steel coffin, as I came to think of it, I had time to think—nothing but time. There was no day, no night, just consuming, unending boredom and a constant attempt to maneuver my naked body into a bearable position to ease the pain of open, raw sores from scraping against the steel walls and rough cement floor with a single drain hole in the center. It took a while before I could see beyond my anger and self-pity to gather my thoughts into any kind of sense. But I had time—time and my thoughts . . .

Introduction

Part I is a revision of the original book (***From A Distance—I Can See God***) offers a reinterpretation of the original title of ***The WILLIAM RAMSEY Story.*** The chapters emerged as the book was reorganized and expanded the Life of William Ramsey story.

Part II includes information about Texas Death row and testimonies of Texas Death Row inmates (both living and executed) with which William Ramsey has worked. It also includes inspirational writings from a young man on probation Bill worked with and helped to avoid prison.

PART I

Life Story of William Ramsey

CHAPTER 1

"Or else . . . the Hole"

"Oh, I didn't start out to be bad—But, isn't that what they all say?"

"Your quota is three-hundred-fifty pounds of cotton a day—every day—or else . . ."

That was my introduction to the Texas Department of Corrections prison work farm. The guard's threat of "Or else . . ." did not bother me. I was a rough, tough twenty-two year old, street-wise kid and had survived my share of fights and beatings. Matter of fact, I went out of my way to start fights. This guard did not scare me.

It was 1965, and I had just arrived at Central Number 1, in Sugar Land, Texas, after spending six months' confinement in the county jail, and I was physically out of shape. Like most of the jail inmates, I had heard the stories of life in prison from guys who had been there. I knew you had to be mean and tough or bad things would happen to you. I figured a few days working in the fields picking cotton would get me hardened up and ready to take care of myself when I got to regular prison.

I wasn't happy about being routed out of my bunk at five in the morning, but we got a pretty good breakfast before they marched us out to the fields to work. It was in June and about six o'clock—just getting light.

They grouped us into squads of anywhere from thirty to forty men each. They called the squads *"hoes"* . . . Hoe number one, Hoe number two, and so on. They assigned me to pick what looked like an endless row of cotton. We were issued a long burlap sack to drag behind us and to fill with cotton. Every so often, the wagon came around to empty our sack and to weigh what we had picked. The sun's heat and the constant stooping to pick the cotton bolls made the perspiration run. I would have soon dehydrated if it were not for the water wagon coming around every couple of hours. Big wooden barrels of tepid water were tapped by a long-handled wooden, ladle-like dipper for us to drink from.

We broke for the noon meal—a good one, fortunately, because it often was to be my last meal of the day. I quickly learned that when darkness fell, if my quota was not picked—350 pounds of cotton—I lost my evening meal and my cot for the night.

My very first day, I managed to pick less than one hundred pounds of cotton. The guard reminded me I was to pick at least three hundred fifty pounds, and ordered me to be taken to "*the Hole*". To this day, I can still see the look of cruel satisfaction on his face. I can remember the sinking feeling in the pit of my stomach; I knew that look. It was the same sort of look my father sometimes got after he had hit or beat me to make a point.

The guards took me to a large room where ten to fifteen iron boxes—each the size of a small 2x2-foot telephone booth—lined the walls. The air hung think and heavy from the heat of the day and reeked with the smell of open sewers and unwashed bodies. There was no air conditioning. I was ordered to strip and, naked as the day I was born, I was locked into the chamber of my worst nightmares.

The darkness closed in around me. I was bewildered by the injustice of it all. After all, they had not caught me; I had turned myself in to the authorities. I had been stealing cars, mostly to joy ride, but also tripping and selling them. I soon found I was not making enough money to support myself. I knew what I was doing; the stealing, vandalism, shoplifting, drinking, carousing and fighting in bars were wrong. I also knew I belonged in jail. At every opportunity, for as long as I could remember, I lived up to my parents' expectations that I "am sorry, no good, and will never amount to anything." My parents often told me I was *"born bad."* I proved them right. Words are powerful, go deep, and shape a person's self-image which shapes his future.

By turning myself in, I expected a light sentence, or at least some measure of understanding and leniency, from the courts. By turning myself in, I hoped to somehow clean the slate and maybe to get a fresh start. But that was not to be. I became an example for the prosecution and was given the maximum sentence allowed by law . . . four years in prison.

The metal sides and cold, rough cement floor of "*the Hole*" allowed no room for comfort—no space to lie down or stretch out my arms. Turning and twisting against the unforgiving metal, I finally wedged myself into as near a position of rest as I could for the duration of the night. I was told they would come for me in the morning to go back to the cotton fields.

The night became one long miserable session, trying to find a position in which I could relax enough to gain the sleep I desperately craved. What little air I had to breathe filtered in through a series of holes drilled in a steep plate near the top of the cell. The smell from the sewer opening in the floor was almost overpowering. My muscles became cramped and sore; my confusion increased; and my anger grew by leaps and bounds. Cursing the system, I let my mind drift back over time and events, trying to figure out what I had done to deserve this . . .

By the time I was ten years old, I learned how to smoke, snitching my mother's Pall Mall cigarettes. I knew if I got caught I would get a beating, but I would get that anyway. At least when they yelled at me or hit me, they were paying attention to me. And, like any kid, that is really all I wanted.

I remember when I was seven or eight years old, for about six weeks straight, my mother dropped me off at church each Sunday, but she never came in with me. Maybe her drinking made her reluctant to enter the church; I don't know. What I do believe is something compelled her to introduce God to me and me to God. It did not work. I could not understand why this just and merciful God everyone at church talked about would let me live in such a painful and unhappy place. It just wasn't fair!

At that time my brother fared no better than I. He, too, felt the wrath of our alcoholic parents. Our sister, *"the apple of their eye"* as they constantly reminded us, received what little affection existed in our home. It was not long before our younger brother was born and he fared somewhat better than us, but he also experienced their wrath.

My middle brother and I had to walk to school no matter what the weather. Thankfully, living in the South, we did not have to content with snow or ice too often. Our sister always was driven to school in the car. She did not want to be seen with us—her rag-tag, always fighting, socially unacceptable brothers. Her hair was always perfectly done and her clothes the latest fashion, while we wore anything we could scrounge together. It just was not fair!!

Thinking back, I cannot remember my brother or me ever having a birthday party like our sister had with her invited friends and their mountains of presents. Whenever she had a party or even if her friends came to visit, we boys were shut in our rooms or shooed outside—not to be seen or acknowledged. If we did not want a beating, we stayed put!

These reflective thoughts made me aware of the cramped, tortuous box in which I found myself trapped. Wistfully, I remembered the freedom of the outdoors as a child. Of course, I did not think of it as freedom then. I was not allowed in the house during the day. My mother kept the doors locked, and I could only come inside in the evenings to eat, take a bath, and go to bed. I got caught in the house when I was about six years old, and my mother picked up a piece of ceramic kitchen tile and threw it at me yelling, *"Get out of the house!"* The tile struck me in the head and I ended up in the hospital emergency room where I received eight stitches in my scalp. My mother told them I had tripped and fallen.

Even after school, I could not enter the house until suppertime. When the weather turned bad, I took refuge under trees, bushes, in garages, barns—anywhere I could—except our house; I was not allowed in there. At times we went to the houses of school friends or simply walked the streets. I would run away to avoid the inevitable beatings, but I always came back. Right now, in *"the Hole,"* even that little freedom seemed like heaven.

I must have dozed off, because the next thing I knew the heavy steel door clanged open and I was ordered out. Shielding my eyes from the painfully bright light, I unfolded my body and stumbled out of my cage. It took what seemed like forever to get my mind oriented and my body straightened out enough to get dressed . . . particularly with the guards yelling and prodding me to hurry up and constantly reminding me I still had three-hundred-fifty pounds of cotton to pick.

Out in the fields, trying my best to pick my quota of cotton, I picked until my fingers were raw. Weak from lack of food and sleep, I didn't even take time for water until my thirst became overpowering. At the end of the day, I had picked even less than the day before.

"Thirty days in 'the Hole'," the guard growled in that cruel tone of voice my parents had introduced me to; then he grinned.

"Thirty days." It hit me like a physical blow as though he had struck me with a hammer. One night had been an eternity; I could not even imagine thirty nights. I was angry and cursed them, so they beat me.

Now too numb to even think, I was marched back into the room with those coffin-like boxes and was ordered to strip. I was too dazed to react to the onslaught of insults and belittling remarks they taunted me with—hoping to get a rise out of me so they could beat me down again. Their remarks cut like lashes and took me back to the all-too-familiar taunts I had endured from my parents.

In drunken hazes, my parents subjected my brother and I to constant degrading, hurtful verbal abuse, and at times, beatings with hands and fists or a stick or belt. Anything movable and handy would do. We were punished into a state of agonizing pain and submission. Many times, my nose was broken by my father's fist, and I can remember crawling off to bed hoping not to get blood on the sheets. I did not want another beating from my mom.

I came to believe the only reason for my existence was to serve them—or anyone in authority, for that matter. This became my lot in life—the only way, I felt, I could gain their attention. I never knew a hug or kind encouraging word from them—only pain—pain which matured and grew into hate and anger to be passed on to those around me. By lashing out and dominating others, I could get the attention I felt I deserved and craved.

There is no way to adequately describe the feeling of despair I felt at the harsh sound of that iron door crashing shut . . . cut off from the world . . . cut off from life.

Again, the anger and injustice took over and consumed me. Time passed. I screamed. I cried. I threw myself against the unmerciful cold steel side of the cell. Fortunately, with so little room in which to maneuver, I could not do much damage to my body. Time had no meaning; there was no day, no night—only unending darkness and the occasional break in the silence by the sound of yelling and cursing and screaming taunts and abuse from my past which echoed off the steel walls to batter my ears—sounds I was not sure if they came from my mouth or mind. Perhaps, it was both.

Occasionally, a narrow slot at the bottom of the door briefly opened, and I received my daily allowance of bread and some water. This was my only sustenance and my only contact with the outside world. I grew to live those few seconds of light which came at infrequent intervals a lifetime apart.

I was born bad. I wanted to punish myself. I deserved to be punished. I wanted to die. I deserved to die. I wanted to punish and kill those who put me here. But, I could do nothing—nothing but crawl back into my garbled mind and await the opening of that bit of sanity at the bottom of my door.

In the darkness, after much soul searching, I finally came to understand I was in a game I could not con my way out of. Hmmm . . . I believe I was born a con man.

CHAPTER 2

Manipulator . . . Con Man

Even as a child, I would manipulate my brother out of his things which I wanted. One Christmas, the only Christmas I can remember my brother and me receiving a gift from my parents, they gave us cheap, chrome plated watches for presents; mine did not even run. I switched watches with my brother. He never knew. When he discovered his watch did not work, he threw it down in disgust and said, *"It's busted! I guess that is all you can expect from them anyway!"*

Being about the same size, I would talk him out of any clothes that were nicer than mine, not that there were many. He didn't seem to care. Looking back, I can see where I developed my talent to manipulate situations and people. If I couldn't talk my way around something, I used my fists, later knives. I loved to fight—to hurt people, to damage or destroy property. It gave me a sense of power, the recognition I so desperately sought. But the steel walls and rough concrete that chafed my sore muscles and raw skin, reminded me that they would not be manipulated by a glib tongue or ready fists.

At some point, in the solitude of that cramped dark cell, I once again began to question just what I had done to deserve this treatment. In my mind I knew I deserved to be here, but I wasn't ready to accept it. On the other hand, my heart told me I did. In fact, I deserved to be here not for failing to pick my quota of cotton—but, for all the lies I had told, all the things I had stolen, all the people I cheated and all the fights I'd started . . . After all, when you do something wrong, you are supposed to be punished. I knew this to be true, because it had been beaten into me by my parents, verbally reminded of it and reinforced by my teachers, and threatened with it by others for as long as I could remember. Yet, my mind told me that if you are deprived of something you think you deserve, you have a right to get it. I wanted recognition, love, friends, and all the things I thought everyone else had. After all, I was entitled to these things, and I was ready, willing, and able to do anything to get them. And I did.

I lost any sense of time. There was no day, no night, no break in the darkness, and except for a rare, occasional slamming of a cell door I heard no sound. I could only wedge myself against the merciless cold metal of my two by two world. Not enough room to sit. I constantly struggled to find a position that would allow me some rest. I never found one. I stood in my own feces and urine. There was no relief—no hope.

And the cockroaches came. After my initial revulsion, I found a strange kinship with them. They became a frail link to reality. They were alive—I was alive . . . proof that I existed and not consigned to some eternal purgatory as my bewildered thoughts feared. I found myself giving the cockroaches names: John, George, Mary, Sam, Betty. I imagined them doing things as a child would play with dolls. We played games; I assigned the beetles numbers and positions, and held races and contests. I told them childhood fairy tales and stories. We lived, and I was surviving.

I had withdrawn into a numbed state and lost all sense of being, when suddenly, the door to my world opened, and through squinted eyes, I welcomed the harsh glare of the morning sun streaming through the high windows. Light never looked so wonderful. Even the disgusted sneers of the guards, held its own beauty for me as I staggered from my cage. I was weak, but after a few wobbly steps, I managed to walk on my own. I was alive.

They prodded me into a shower room where they hosed me down with a high-pressure hose and even the stinging jet of water was gladly endured. After drying as best I could with a coarse towel, they threw me some clothes and with their constant taunts, forced me to the dining area to eat. This was the first solid food I had seen in thirty days. Pasty oatmeal, cold scrambled powdered eggs, burnt dry toast, and it all tasted like ambrosia. It seemed no sooner had I sat down to eat; we were marching to the fields where I was still expected to pick my quota of three-hundred-fifty pounds of cotton.

I didn't make it past mid-morning. I was physically bankrupt—too weak to continue, although I tried. The guards, on horseback, herded me like a sick calf back to *"the Hole"* and ordered me to strip, then shoved me back into Hell. It had not even been hosed out as they were supposed to do.

I didn't believe I could last another thirty days in that hole—it was unfathomable. I was being put back in there to die, surely as if they were executing me. Once again, darkness, silence and an unknown will to survive became my existence.

Like the bottomless pit of Hell, time stretched into forever. Periodically, an overpowering stench seeped into the darkness that made me retch with the dry heaves. The odious smell came from the open sewer hole at my feet, through the tiny air holes at the top of my prison, saturating the air with the smell of death. This odor emanated from prisoners who had died and were left in "*the Hole*" to rot until their punishment time was up; then the guards came to get them. I believed I was next. By order of the "Bosses", dead or alive, you served the full time.

Driven by the seemingly never-ending pain of open sores covering my face, back, knees, shoulders and arms, my mind turned to dark thoughts of death. Those festering wounds from the constant contact with the rough walls and floor of my tiny world became my torturous universe. I tried to pray, to bargain with God, if there was one, for my release from the misery and suffering I had been forced into. I wanted to die. I wondered if there was a Heaven or Hell. And if there were such places, where was I going? I just asked God, *"You know that I'd like to go to Heaven. I wanted to go there."*

I had heard people speak of prayer and salvation and peace, but those things were foreign to me. I knew the words, but I had no idea what they meant or how to achieve them. I tried to recall some of the prayers the preacher had offered in those distant times my mother had dropped me off at Sunday school. They wouldn't come. From childhood, the only prayer I could remember was *"Now I lay me down to sleep . . ."* and I could neither lie down nor sleep.

I thought I was going to die. I rehashed all the things I had done to deserve being punished like this. I pondered about what had made me such a disobedient child, then adult. I tried, in vain, to reason out why I took the road I did, instead of being like other people. It was as though I was trying to live the script my parents had laid out for me—I was nothing, and would "*never amount to anything.*" Time wore into nothingness. Even the cockroaches no longer gave meaning to my existence. For interminably long stretches, my mind shut down and refused to function. Wedged into a crouched position with my knees to my chest, I lost myself in the sharp, red pain of just being . . . just existing.

Occasionally, my link to the outside at the bottom of the door slid back and my ration of bread and cup of water were shoved inside. When the impact of that brief flash of light would awaken me from those long periods of nothingness, I was never sure whether I had or had not eaten. I had no idea of how many rations I missed. In those periods of consciousness, my thoughts turned back to begging, pleading, bargaining, and praying for release from my aching body in the same manner I remembered begging my parents for relief of the physical and emotional pain inflicted on me as a child.

I remembered the picture of Jesus Christ, and God, from childhood picture books—the long white flowing robes and the serene faces. The picture of Jesus in a beautiful white robe became my focus. At that point a soft, warm serenity overcame me. I no longer felt the excruciating pain of my wounds. I could see a place of bright light and peace—a place where I could feel no pain and be serene and free from the ruined carcass that housed my soul. I know now it was, in fact, God relieving me of the pain I could no longer bear.

I have no conception of how long this state lasted, but abruptly the cell door clanked open and a booming voice said, "*Okay, scum, your ninety days are up!*" Ninety days! How could have ninety days passed?

I truly believe this miracle spared my life. Many rotted and died in that hole, but that was not the plan God had for me.

My eyes squeezed shut at the harsh, bright light. I tried to move, but I couldn't. My body was frozen in a fetal position, with my back against the wall. I felt rough hands grab me and drag me onto the concrete floor of the building. Weak, near death, I couldn't speak. I opened my mouth to scream from the pain, but no sound came out. They hosed me off with the pressure hose used to clean the cells and fiery agony wracked me from the gangrenous puss-filled sores that covered my body. They finally straightened my limbs enough to slide me into some clothes and called for the medics to carry me to the prison hospital.

At the prison hospital they ripped the clothes (now glued to my skin by the blood and puss from the open wounds) from my gaunt body. Again, and again, I tried to scream to protest, but sound would not come. The pain became more than I could bear, and the last thing I remembered was the medic saying, *"The damn scale only shows him at ninety pounds, I doubt he'll last until morning."*

Welcomed darkness overtook me.

CHAPTER 3

More Dead than Alive . . .
I Learned to Survive

In contrast to *"the Hole,"* the prison hospital seemed like heaven. The first thing I noticed when I came to was the smell—clean, bright, and fresh. Most important, it wasn't reeking of the sewer, and the air wasn't sweltering hot or freezing cold. It almost killed me when they finished ripping my clothes off.

I simply lay there like a rag doll—unable to walk or speak, more vegetable than human. At that point, cocooned in my own world, more dead than alive, I was beyond caring if I lived or not. From my robust 185-pound weight, I had become a scant 90 pound skin covered skeleton. Immediately an IV was put into my arm to start building up my strength. My painful abrasions were cleaned, treated and dressed. But the mental and physical agony was with me constantly.

The days passed, and it wasn't long before I was able to stand and take a few wobbly steps. I had to retrain my legs to respond, even to accomplish a simple thing like walking. Still I could not communicate, carry on a conversation beyond a very basic level. A speech therapist was brought in to teach me how to speak again. The hospital orderlies were all inmates, and they took good care of you. Not like the *"Bosses"*, as we called, *"our keepers,"* who, it seemed, would try to provoke you into doing something rash so they had an excuse to discipline you. Six weeks of constant care and speech therapy in the hospital and I was released back into the general prison population—physically, but not mentally healed. I still carried the rage and hatred inside of me.

I was first assigned to being a building tender at the farm unit. Instead of cells, we lived in large open barracks lined with cots. The barrack buildings were arranged like spokes on a wheel with the guard station in the middle, and each spoke called a wing. With about a hundred men to a wing, the prisoners were strictly segregated, Blacks with Blacks, Hispanics with Hispanics and Whites with Whites. When everyone else on my wing went to work on the farm and other various jobs, my job as tender was to sweep and mop the floors and keep the area clean. I also gave the other inmates haircuts. You didn't need formal barber training because there was only one acceptable hairstyle. I just had to run the clippers over their heads until there was nothing but skin. Hair was not allowed.

It wasn't long before my strength began to return and I was assigned to work in the laundry . . . a job I held for the rest of my time in Sugar Land prison. Laundry work was a regular eight-hour a day grueling job, without pay. It was a large facility, doing all the laundry for the prison population, an enormous task. With no air conditioning, in the winter the laundry became a haven to keep warm, in the summer, however, it turned into an inferno with the unbearable heat generated by the boilers, washers and steam presses, but I had no choice. I did not want to give the "*Bosses*" the tiniest excuse to send me back to "*the Hole.*"

Life in prison became a constant struggle for survival. At each turn you learned to be careful what you said and to whom you said it. My speech patterns became guarded so I wouldn't give offense to anyone . . . a Boss or a fellow prisoner. Fights were frequent and punishment harsh—sometimes deadly.

One morning, I awoke to find a cellmate in the bunk next to mine dead. Pinned to his cot by a shank, a homemade knife made from a stolen piece of metal, stuck completely through him and the mattress. I had heard nothing during the night—even if I had, I wouldn't have said anything or I would be the next victim not to awaken. Later in the day, I was told he died because of an argument over some tobacco. My cellmate lost his life because he had not paid back a pack of Bugler tobacco he owed someone.

Another time, while hoeing crops in the farm fields, a dispute was settled by an inmate quickly stepping over a row of vegetables while the guards were occupied and striking the fellow in front of me with his hoe, then stepping back and continuing his work as if nothing had happened. The blow pealed back the entire back of the skull, and he turned to me and asked what happened. I told him he had just been killed. Without another sound, he crumpled to the ground, dead. When asked what occurred, I explained I didn't know—I had been working. *"Hear no evil, see no evil,"* and certainly if you valued your life, you *"spoke no evil."* You quickly learned to bury any outward display of emotion.

We were allowed fourteen dollars every two weeks in the commissary. If you had anyone on the outside, they could send you money and you would be issued stamps, like food stamps, which could be spent in the commissary. You did without. We were furnished a bag of Bull Durham tobacco and some papers to roll it in, but that's all. Everyone hated to roll cigarettes, so if you didn't have any money to buy some of your own, you sometimes could earn smokes by rolling a bunch of cigarettes for other prisoners. Bumming or borrowing anything from other inmates without repayment was unacceptable. Life in prison was cheap.

Things like a pencil, a pen, a real cigarette, became items of life and death importance. Your word was sacred, and if you failed to honor it, retribution was unsympathetic and swift for those that didn't bend to the system. I developed what the psychiatrists call, *'a f—it, I don't care,'* attitude. Between the verbal and sometimes physical abuse from the *"Bosses"* and the constant threat from the prisoners, you learned prison etiquette in a hurry, or you didn't come out alive. I learned to survive.

Coming from a totally unstructured environment on the outside, I now found myself part of a completely structured one. We were told when to go to bed, when to get up; when to shower; when to eat; when to go to the bathroom; when to sit and when to stand—when to speak and when to be silent. I had forsaken my freedom to become a puppet, whose strings were controlled by people and events outside of me. At first it was maddening, then degrading, and my resentment and disregard for the justice system grew. But, I learned to survive.

Life in prison wasn't all bad, although it certainly seemed that way most of the time. It was a learned experience; we constantly gained small victories by developing new ways to outwit the *"Bosses"*, to get away with things forbidden. We had plenty of mind-numbing alcohol to help us tolerate our dismal conditions and even more dismal futures. Home brew, made from apple juice or other fruit or berries and sugar stolen from the kitchen. Hidden in corners, beneath bunks, and out of the way areas, could always be found jars, bottles, cans, or buckets filled with fermenting juice. Periodically, the guards would run a shakedown to search out and destroy the potent drink, but we always made more. We got drunk, and we existed.

Drugs were occasionally smuggled in; there were courier systems, bribed officials and clandestine drops, to obtain almost anything you desired from the outside—if you had the money to pay for it. Drugs weren't as prevalent as today, but while in prison was the first time I was exposed to and tried them. I didn't particularly care for them then. Drug addicts were considered outcasts, pariahs to be shunned, and the lowest of the low. I didn't want, nor could I socially afford, to be associated with them. I learned to survive.

The long awaiting day finally came and I gained parole. Freedom!

By the Grace of God, I survived.

CHAPTER 4

Freedom at Last—Only to Return

Freedom . . . I can't begin to tell you what it felt like to be released back into the open world . . . free to do and say what I wanted; free to come and go as I pleased; free to talk to and be with a woman; free to drink liquor openly—all without fear of reprisal from the *"Bosses"* or fellow prisoners.

The conditions of my release were designed in some measure to protect me from myself—reporting to my parole officer, getting a job, not associating with known criminals.

I chose to ignore them. One of the first things I did was head for a bar where I could talk, laugh and drink without a Boss standing over me and telling me what I could and could not do. I was free.

Not long after I hit the streets, I met a girl who became my constant companion, both in and out of bed. Finally, after my hellish existence in prison for the past two years, I believed I had paid my debt to society, and I had a willing young lady by my side. It seemed like absolute heaven, but Satan himself shadowed my every footstep.

I was mad at the world. I drank. I fought. I cursed the system and the people in it.

Three months of freedom and my parole was revoked, my girlfriend was pregnant, and I was sent back to prison to complete my four-year term.

When it came to my behavior I was a slow learner, but I learned. Back in prison there were more fights, more inmates being killed around me, more *"Bosses"* telling me what I could and could not do, and when to do it. But, I learned. I *"kept my nose clean,"* and I finished my sentence.

My girlfriend, whom I left pregnant, met me at the gate with a daughter I had never seen. I had twenty-five dollars, a loud Hawaiian shirt, and a pair of khaki pants. But I learned.

Because of the baby, my girlfriend's mother ordered (at the point of a shotgun) that we get married. It was truly a shotgun wedding. Even though I had no intention, nor wanted to, we got married. I had just been released from prison with no job and no future, yet her mother insisted.

Strangely, something happened inside of me. I was now a father, and I wanted to straighten out my life. Times were hard at first, but I landed a job in La Port, Texas, at a chemical plant where I started at the bottom of the ladder with a renewed determination to work my way up—to make a good life for my new wife and our child.

The fact it was a chemical plant was important to me in as much as I was following in the footsteps of my father and brothers with a job in a chemical plant. I suddenly found myself trying to prove to my parents that I was worthy of their praise—I would and could succeed in spite of what they had always told me. I had been raised to believe I was worthless and better off out of their lives, because I would never amount to anything.

On the job I drove myself, volunteering for overtime, doing jobs no one wanted. In less than three years, I steadily advanced from clearing weeds along the railroad tracks to become a supervisor . . . a position my father never attained in all the years he worked in the plants. Not once did my parents ever tell me they were proud of me nor that I had done well. I wore their scorn and rejection like an anchor around my neck.

Soon, married life and the everyday struggle to pay bills and maintain a household became another weight I wasn't willing to put up with. I sought solace in the bars and beer joints after work, attempting to numb the monotonous reality of my life. Temptation was truly laid in my path, and I was continually tripped up by it. My drinking increased and I started seeking a different solace and approval in the arms of other women.

I would stay out until wee hours carousing, drinking, and spending a few drunken minutes or hours in strange motel rooms or bedrooms with ladies plucked from life's apple tree of temptation. I constantly had to prove that I was not worthless, that I was a person, a real man. I would stagger home to face a bitter argument with my waiting wife before having to catch a little sleep and report for work the next morning.

Before long I, along with others, discovered the seeming unlimited supplies of ethyl alcohol used in the chemical refining process. Before it was laced with benzene, a poison with a distinctive color and odor to prevent anyone from drinking it, we would siphon a bit of each barrel to drink. It was pure alcohol, two-hundred-proof grain alcohol. It was free, and we drank it and my addiction to *"demon rum"* increased. Every bit of the alcohol had to be accounted for, but records were falsified to make up for some of the loss and the rest could be accounted for through spillage and evaporation. I suspect the practice still goes on in most manufacturing plants where ethyl alcohol is used. For someone who has a craving for alcohol, the temptation is too great to ignore.

I was never good with managing money, and we lived in one apartment after another, but finally managed to buy a home under the GI bill. The payments were one hundred forty-nine dollars a month. It became a constant drain of money and energy just to maintain it. Meanwhile, the drinking and partying continued. The money didn't go far when I was spending it on alcohol and women other than my wife. In less than a year I defaulted on the house, and not knowing any better, I allowed it to be repossessed. I moved my family back into the low rent apartments.

Our second child, another daughter, came along and then a third. Each additional responsibility forged another link in my anchor's chain, a ready-made sympathetic excuse to the already heavy burden that served as my reason to drink and run around. Each new responsibility not only added to my concerns of providing, but more importantly, they restricted my freedom. After my period of confinement in prison, freedom had become all-important to me. Constantly strapped for money, I buried myself deeper into the drinking along with occasionally smoking marijuana and taking pills to alleviate the anguish and pain that grew inside of me.

The fights at home increased in length and intensity, fortunately only verbally and not physically violent. One of the things in my life I often boasted of is the fact I was never physically abusive to women. I have since learned the power of mere words can wield the force of a whip, or club, or a knife cutting deep into the soul of a person, and I used words indiscriminately. My boasts fell on deaf ears.

One of the few constants in my life, other than women and alcohol, was my motorcycle, a Harley Davidson. It became my symbol of freedom—my statement I could do what I wanted when I wanted. The people that ran with the motorcycle gangs were a freewheeling, tough, group of individuals always ready for a fight. A carefree bunch with lots of alcohol, drugs, and sex wherever and whenever you wanted and this was a life-style, which on evenings and weekends I adopted as my own.

For thirteen years I lived this façade of married life providing for my family and being the breadwinner and good husband. Then one unfortunate afternoon I discovered my wife and another man in a compromising situation, in bed. In an uncontrollable rage, I beat them both up—mostly him, putting him in the hospital. Her behavior was completely unknown to me and left me devastated. It was all right for me to cheat and run around, but it was certainly not all right for my wife to do the same. I never learned how long it had been going on, but I suspected for quite some time.

I left and went to my parents' home and then checked myself into a hospital to repair the hernia I had got from kicking down my wife's bedroom door. The anger still burned through me and they finally had to give me medication to calm me down. I was having a nervous breakdown. Shortly after that when my wife filed for divorce, I didn't contest it; I wanted nothing except my motorcycle and freedom.

Along the way, I met a twenty-year old girl, Diana, who made me feel like a king. At thirty-seven, my ego fed upon the rapt attention she paid me and we started living together. She liked to do all the things I liked: drinking, going to clubs, smoking marijuana and of course, sex. It became a glorious life of debauchery doing whatever we wanted, when we wanted as long as it made us feel good. I sank deeper into the Devil's snake pit.

We would occasionally visit her parents, and one thing that impressed me was the fact her parents, devout Christians, always seemed happy and satisfied with their lives. I wasn't sure what to make of that, but it appealed to me. They had something I wanted—normal existence with the unqualified approval of their family and friends. Over and over I asked Diana if she wanted to change her life around, to start going to church and quit doing drugs and liquor—she didn't. Neither did I, but the seed had been planted.

I was still filled with rage and anger—at what or whom, I didn't know. I found the devil's power in being able to hurt people. It made me feel more like a man. When riding with the motorcycle gang, I was called *"the dentist"*. If someone rubbed us the wrong way or wasn't obedient, several of the others would hold them down and I would pull a tooth with a pair of pliers. I pulled many teeth. With every tooth came a sense of belonging, acceptance, and a measure of respect from the others in the gang. There was safety in numbers and we were all bullies.

On another occasion, in a bar one night, a man, not of our gang, was paying too much attention to my woman. He would put his hand on her body, and I would tell him to keep his hands off of her. Finally, he turned to pick up his drink from the bar, I whipped out a knife I habitually carried at my side, and the fight was on.

Fights were legendary—knives, guns, and fists. There weren't many who stood against us. Those that did were soon beaten into submission. A lot of gunshots were fired during these free-for-alls, but I never saw anyone get hit. On the other hand, many carry physical scars from the knives and mental scars from my actions. I rejoiced in the notoriety and felt myself accepted by the members of the gang. They gave me the respect I wanted but never received from my parents.

It wasn't long before the *"good life"* began wearing thin, and I wanted something more. I quit my job, moved out, and left town. I kept in contact with Diana, but it wasn't too long before she overdosed on drugs and ended up in a coma and became a living vegetable. She created her own purgatory—lying in a sanitarium in that not-alive but not-quite dead state for about five years. She passed away in the early 1990s. Just think . . . It could have been me.

I firmly believe back when I had asked Diana if we could go to church and try to change, that was a choice we had to make. Evidently, each of us already had made a decision—not consciously, but in our hearts. She chose to continue her path of destruction that led to death and received worse. I chose to leave town, still seeking the answer to an unknown question that gnawed at my being. Now, I firmly believe God saw what was in our hearts and granted each of our desires. I think we sometimes make choices without even realizing it.

Totally disillusioned with my lot in life, I took to the road and a life I had been programming myself for all along: the life I knew best, a life of no responsibility; life with plenty of liquor, drugs, and willing women; a life of freedom to do what I wanted, when I wanted. Also, I discovered, it was a life to be miserable, depressed, lonely and unsatisfying—a life that could only lead to insanity or death. It was times like these that my thoughts returned to Diana's parents and the happiness they enjoyed in the folds of their church and God. I often wondered about it but wasn't willing to change my lifestyle to attain that elusive thing they had.

Yet, I returned to the ways of survival—lying, stealing, cheating, doing anything necessary to bury and mask the pain I felt inside of my heart. The rejection of my family and my own lack of any self-worth drove me deeper into alcohol and drugs, which became a life I understood and embraced. I ran with friends of a like nature—misfits of society, operating outside the laws of man and God. I know now, it was Satan's own horde I ran with.

CHAPTER 5

Finding Real Purpose for My Life

Broke, discouraged and angry—
But found the real purpose for my life!

As always, drawn back to my roots, I returned to the area of southeast Texas where my family lived. Broke, discouraged, I was angry at the world for my sorry plight, and I was mad at God for burdening me with parents who refused to acknowledge I was anything but worthless. My life had become a screwed up mess. I lashed out at anyone and anything that stood in my way of finding comfort. I didn't like what was happening to me, but I couldn't change. I blamed everyone but myself.

Alcohol and drugs numbed the pain I felt and made living bearable for a time. By this time I was thoroughly addicted. I could not stop drinking and doing drugs. I took a job in a bar where I could drink as much as I wanted and associate with the kind of people I understood.

I took a room near the bar where I worked, but soon found myself looking for something more in my life. I got a job with a chemical construction company that would enable me to direct my life up and out of the pit I had dug for myself. I tried to find for myself some of the peace and happiness I saw in others like Diana's church-going parents.

My parents would not let me live with them, so I was forced to find somewhere else to live. Apartments were expensive. I finally found an affordable room in a boarding house in a nice part of town. Denise, the lady who ran it, was a devout Christian and laid down strict guidelines about drinking and drugs; but this presented no problem. I simply lied to her. I wasn't about to give up the things I needed most. One of the things I needed most at that time was a place where I could afford to stay.

Denise had a young daughter I grew to love—I think, because of the innocence of children like her—and she accepted me for myself, not for what I did or was. However, I was very careful not to drink or do drugs around her for fear she would tell her mother and I would get kicked out.

After a time, in my sodden, scheming mind, I wanted to marry Denise, because I felt she could help me. I was attracted to, but certainly not in love with her. I didn't know how to love her. Yet, there was something about her lifestyle that I saw and never had; but that was okay as long as it suited my purpose at the time. After all, divorce and leaving women was nothing new to me. I had left my first wife several times, and left my second (a common-law wife) who was only with me because we had a mutual interest in alcohol, drugs and sex, not love. Loving someone was foreign to my thinking. I had never received love nor given love to my previous wives or more importantly, to myself.

There was something different about Denise from the other women I had known. She attended church and prayed which brought back childhood memories of when my mother would drop me off at the church on Sundays. I always associated going to church with abandonment; yet, I had vague memories of the church-going people—happy people. I saw something of those happy people in Denise, and I pressed her to marry me. In return, Denise saw something in me beyond what I was, and agreed to marry me, with the stipulation I continue attending church with her. I agreed.

This was against everything I understood and wanted to do, but it was what she wanted. After we were married, she took me to church and brought Bible studies into our home, praying to change my life-long patterns. Never for a minute did she doubt I would be saved. I tried my best to prove her wrong—to give in to my old habits, but it only made her pray harder.

Time after time, I went on drunken binges, stealing her money, everything she carefully saved for our future, and left home for days and weeks on end—only coming back to Denise when my money ran out or I was too sick to continue. Each time she took me back and forgave me. I couldn't understand why. Upon each of my returns, she demanded I go through detoxification and treatment and continue going to church with her. I did as she asked. I felt as though I had no choice, yet, another side of me wanted very much to get my life straightened out.

I learned respect for this tenacious lady, and with it came love and acceptance not only for Denise, but for myself. However, probably the most important thing I learned was an undivided love and respect for Jesus Christ.

Once I found and accepted God's love and forgiveness, I could then begin to forgive my own faults and learn to channel them into help for others, thereby helping myself.

Through the love of Denise and her daughter, I was able to start the healing process. More importantly, through the unconditional love and unqualified acceptance of God, I learned to accept myself. ONLY then, could I help others. Before, I had only known how to abuse others as well as myself . . . abuse by my drinking, by me taking drugs, and abuse toward anyone who stood in my way or that I felt didn't show enough respect to me—even though I never tried to earn it.

Patient, loving care from my wife and her firm belief in God placed my feet on the path for the Miracle of God's love to overtake me. When we first met, I couldn't stand for Denise, or anyone for that matter, to physically touch me, but she dared to. I had never been touched in this way. Being touched represented a repressed pain I didn't want to deal with.

She saw a side of me that I was not aware existed—my love of children and animals. It was she, with her unwavering belief, who started to teach me about affection and finally love. She would always compliment me on various things, even things like the way my hair was combed. She was always positive, never negative.

She saw the way I reacted to her daughter with patience and caring when around her. Maybe instinctively, I found a kinship with one who had come from an abusive father. Yet, in looking back, I could never be comfortable with a child, any child, being injured, not even spanked for disciplinary reasons. This child I adopted as my own when she was only four years old. She taught me about self-esteem and love. She used to tell everyone, *"Daddy could fix anything."* Although hard, I finally started believing her. This was a first for me.

Denise set about to teach me about love—a concept completely unknown to my experience. More than that, so familiar, I wanted to run from it. My acceptance and ability to love didn't happen overnight. It took years . . . years of agony and patience and nurturing by Denise for me to finally be able to recognize it and come to take it as my own.

During those years, Denise couldn't understand why she could love me, and why I had to run away and become this other person—to be what I had always thought of as the *"true me"*. That *"me"*, I now understand, is Satan, living and destroying souls through others and myself who act in this manner. Time after time, she would touch or hug me, and I would shrug it off, generally with some rather harsh words to stop it.

In my mind, I couldn't allow myself to get too close to her—I was convinced she would cast me aside or hate me like everyone else in my past had done. I wasn't about to let that sort of pain into my life once again. I was my own person—even though I really didn't like myself at all. But always, in the back of my mind, I wondered about the people whom I saw that were happy and laughing, at ease with themselves and others. They had something I wanted—and I resented I did not have it.

Like the training of a puppy, Denise, with God's hand, slowly, patiently, taught me to allow, even want, her loving touches and affections. She taught me to hug and be hugged, to love and to be loved. Through her and my new little daughter, God's love taught me that is was alright to love and be loved because I am a person with worth. Furthermore, with God's love, I can pass it on to others—to find and have the same wonderful joy I have found.

With her tender loving care, came a sense of well-being and relief. After my last binge, one of the worst, I came crawling home to Denise and to an experience I can only describe as a miracle. An anger-calming relief and peace came to me when

I finally made Jesus Christ the Lord of my life. I can't explain how it works or how and why it happened to me after all I had done and been; but it happened. I had smoked three packs of cigarettes and drank at least a half-gallon of alcohol a day, but the craving for cigarettes, mind-altering drugs, and alcohol was lifted from me like an opaque curtain. I was able to wake in the morning with a clear head and face the day with my head lifted. I was able to communicate with people, and witness to them what the Lord had done for me—something in my wildest dreams, I would have never imagined doing.

I now know that God was working on me through my wife Denise, my baby daughter, Christina, and the rest of my precious children. He did, in fact, have a purpose for me in this life.

RECAP OF PART I

Part I is part of the Life Story of William Ramsey. It shares some of my life experiences, especially those dealing with a wild, out-of-control life of poor choices, alcohol, drugs, and misusing women. Many of these life experiences led to time spent in prison life, which is also captured in a few chapters.

With all my heart, I regret all of the terrible things I have done, and mourn the people I have injured, but I cannot change what was done. I have no one to blame but myself. Yet, if I had not lived my life as I did, I couldn't hope to help those still living in the pits of Hell make peace with God, with others, and with themselves.

Subsequently, I received my certification and worked as a Chaplain Intern in the prison system to help bring the wonderful peace and serenity I found to those who still are in the terrible grasp of Satan.

Deuteronomy 28:15-68 describes the first forty-nine years of my life, because of the curses spoken over me, and choices I made. Now, I praise God, and am living out *Deuteronomy 28:1-14*, under God's Blessing.

There is hope for any and all who want to accept Jesus Christ as their Lord and Savior. He will do for you what he did for me. Make Christ your choice. Why wait another day? Why not does it now?

PART II

Testimonies
Of
Prisoners
And Others
Spared from Prison
By
Bill Sharing
His Life in Christ

CHAPTER 6

Texas Death Penalty Facts

Texas "Firsts"

- Texas is **first in the number of executions** carried out in the United States since 1976. From December 7, 1982 through June 1, 2011, 468 persons have been executed in Texas. Three of those were females: Karla Faye Tucker in 1998, one white female in 2000, and one black female in 2005. California, Florida, and Texas have the largest death row populations.

- Texas was the **first** state in the United States to carry out an execution **by lethal injection**, executing Charles Brooks on December 7, 1982.

- **Karla** was convicted of murder in Texas in 1984 and put to death in 1998. She was the **first woman to be executed** in the United States since 1984, and the first in Texas since 1863.

Texas Death Row History

From 1928 to 1952, death row was located in the East Building of the Huntsville Unit, and the electric chair was located in a building by the East Wall of the Huntsville Unit from 1952 until 1965. In 1965, the men on death row were moved from the Huntsville Unit to the Ellis Unit in Huntsville TX. Death row was moved to the Polunsky Unit in Livingston TX in 1999. There each inmate has a windowed cell about 6'x10'. Women on death row are at the Mountain View Unit in Gatesville TX.

Hanging was the means of execution between 1819 and 1923—carried out by local counties. In 1923, the State of Texas authorized the use of the electric chair that was used until July 30, 1964. A total of 361 inmates were electrocuted in Texas during this period.

Capital punishment was declared "cruel and unusual punishment" by the U.S. Supreme Count on June 29, 1972. The 45 men then on death row in TX and 7 in county jails all had their sentences commuted to life imprisonment.

In 1973, the Texas Penal Code once again allowed assessment of the death penalty and allowed for executions to resume effective January 1, 1974. The means of execution adopted by Texas in 1977 is lethal injection. Effective January 12, 1996, close relatives and friends of the person to be executed were allowed to witness the process.

Throughout the United States five methods of execution are used: lethal injection, electrocution, lethal gas, hanging, and firing squad.

Texas Capital Offenses

The following crimes are Capital Murder in Texas and call for the death penalty: murder of a public safety officer or firefighter; murder during the commission of kidnapping, burglary, robbery, aggravated sexual assault, arson, obstruction, or retaliation; murder for remuneration; murder during prison escape; murder of a correctional employee; murder by a state prison inmate who is serving a life sentence for any of five offenses (murder, capital murder, aggravated kidnapping, aggravated sexual assault, or aggravated robbery); multiple murders; and murder of an individual under six years of age.

Other Interesting Facts

Average time on death row: 10.6 years.

Shortest time on death row: 252 days (1996), 263 days (1998).

Longest time on death row: 709 days (2007), 612 days (2010).

Average age of executed offenders: 39 years.

Youngest at time of execution: 24 years (1985, 1986, and 2002).

Oldest at time of execution: 64 (2003) & 66 (2002).

Texas has the Law of Parties, which allows offenders to be sentenced to death if present while a capital crime is being committed based on the offender being *"criminally responsible for the conduct of another."*

Thirteen juveniles were executed in Texas before the 2005 U.S. Supreme Court decision in Roper v. Simmons. Twenty-nine juveniles awaiting execution were sentenced to Life in Prison and removed from death row in response to the decision.

Although the U.S. Supreme Court prohibited the application of the death penalty to persons with mental retardation in Atkins v. Virginia (2002), the Texas Legislature still has not enacted statutory provisions governing the standards and procedures to be followed in these cases. Texas is still sentencing to death and executing people who may, in fact, be mentally retarded.

True Stories

What you are about to read are true stories written by Texas Death Row inmates and others in danger of going to prison who wanted their stories told after they had committed their lives to Christ.

These inmates and others had a message to tell and wanted to tell the reasons why they were in prison and ways to prevent the same thing from happening to you. They were willing to be candid about their lives in hopes that their stories might prevent someone else from following the same paths as they did.

William Ramsey ministered to many of these inmates and he and his wife, Denise, still minister to prisoners. These inmates shared with William and Denise their desire to get their messages out, especially to young people who have many hard choices to make in this challenging world.

CHAPTER 7

Karla

M_y name is Karla Faye. I was born and raised in Houston, Texas and am currently one of four women housed on Texas' death row. I'm about to share with you some of the wrong choices I made in my life. I'm sure some of you will be able to relate to certain areas real well. In sharing this, my prayer is that somehow, some way, it will reach out and grab some of you who need a good shaking up and make you step back and examine the road you are choosing to follow. There are extremely hard prices that will inevitably be paid if you choose to continue taking this road. There's a much better way in life than the way I chose. My choices led me to death row. Just remember, the choice is indeed yours.

Big and bad and not caring about what others thought or felt—that was me—or so I thought it was, and I wanted everybody else to think so, too.

Up until the age of about eight or nine, I led a fairly normal life. I had a mother and father who worked, two older sisters (I was the epitome of the baby BRAT sister!) and a family dog. We lived in a nice house in an upper middle class neighborhood. We also had a lake house and a boat, and we all went as one big, happy family on weekends, *holidays, and vacations and had a blast. We had all we needed and most of what we wanted. Things were good, but not for long.*

By the time I was ten years old my parents were divorced and we girls were living with my father. This was hard to deal with—three girls living without their mother. What made it even worse was that by the time I was ten, I was also a drug user. At age seven I started smoking cigarettes; by eight or nine I was smoking pot; and by the ripe old age of ten, I was shooting heroine into my veins—and anything else that was fixable! Now I could try and blame the era or my parents for divorcing or even my two sisters since, after all, they were the ones I first smoke pot with. But the fact is, I wanted to do the drugs; I chose to do the drugs. This started a downhill fall for me that eventually led me right here to death row.

Now, you may be thinking that you do drugs and you *are not sliding downhill. Well, you may not realize or recognize it right now, but it is happening. Drugs, alcohol or any other mind-altering substance can either really quickly or over a period of time make a person lose all inhibitions, morals, self-respect, and the list goes on. Believe me, I know!*

I wasn't a big kid, but I was a tomboy to the core. For a girl I was very wiry, agile, very competitive, and uncommonly strong. This got me into a lot of trouble along the way. I had a reputation for being able to street-fight like a bull, and I was always *being challenged. I never lost a fight. I tell you this to reveal the violence induced in me by drugs and alcohol. I seriously hurt many people. I thought fighting was fun, that there was power in being able to use my fists and feet to maul people and hospitalize them. Drugs also caused me to lose all sexual inhibitions and by the time I was thirteen I was sexually active with a capital "A". I was known as* The One *to go to if someone needed sex, drugs, or someone whipped up on. I enjoyed having this to reputation (or so I told myself) and I did all I could to uphold it over the years. I* used sex, drugs and violence to be popular, to control other people, and to feel in control of my own life.

At the age of thirteen I was also exposed somewhat to the "underworld." I became fascinated with their rules, their ethics, and their "street code of a character." I wanted to live by this code, these rules. This certainly didn't help the violent, drug-abusive person I was becoming. It only added to my demented thought processes. As the years went by, I got kicked out of school over and over again for fighting (even with my teachers), for being high in class and falling asleep, and for other reasons. By the time I was mid-way into fifteen I was through with school for good. I walked out and was never made to go back. I became more and more violent and got into all kinds of sexual activities. I toured all over the country with a rock band. I've been strung out and kicked more dope habits than I can count! It was a never-ending cycle. I even harbored sick dreams along the way, like becoming a Mafia hit woman. <u>SICK!</u>

The whole time I was steadily building up walls around me. I used and abused people to satisfy #1—myself. If someone got in my way, I didn't hesitate to bulldoze over him or her. I guess my mother was the only one I ever really allowed to know me, and that wasn't fully. I even had a best friend for fifteen years, and we were closer than Siamese twins. But in retrospect I can also see where I used her to make myself look and feel better. My mother died when I was nineteen and it shattered my whole life. She was everything to me and as a result of her death; I turned stone cold to the world and added about ten more feet to my wall. I had married when my mother died, I left my husband, quit the best job I'd ever had, and was ready to hit the world head on and <u>enjoy</u>. I was free of all men and obligations (or so this was my way of thinking); I had become a high-class call girl and had all the money I thought I needed; no ties to anyone or anything. I thought it couldn't get any better. I was in the gutter hurting everyone that knew and loved me and I didn't even know it.

Then I met a man that I fell in love with and thought could fulfill all my dreams—even the SICK ones. And so we began our trek as mates and in trying to start a training system to become assassins for the "underworld."

Now I don't know if I really would have become a hit woman, but people let me tell you, because of my choice to do drugs, I had indeed lost all inhibitions, morals, scruples, love, self-respect, and, as I stated earlier, the list goes on. What it boils down to is this: I made a conscious choice to do these drugs and as a result I did in fact end up helping to take two precious lives. Not as an assassin but that's beside the point.

I tried blaming my mother for dying on me. I tried blaming drugs; I even tried blaming society. But the simple fact is, I made the choices. We all get to the age of accountability and know right from wrong. We must take responsibility for our own actions!

By the time I was twenty-three, there I sat in the County Jail waiting to be tried for capital murder. It was there, in 1983, that I made another choice—the best choice I've ever made in my whole life. A Christ-centered outreach group called Teen Challenge came to the jail and after seeing them, I chose to give my life to Jesus Christ! I accepted Jesus as my personal Lord and Savior, and my whole life changed for the better! Oh, I still got the death sentence, but that didn't matter. My personal relationship with Jesus gave me an inner peace and joy I had never felt before. From time to time over the years it gets really, really rough, but Jesus never said it would be easy. In fact, He said "there would be tribulation but not to worry because He overcame the world". In the hard times Jesus promised to give me strength and peace and He has never failed me!

There are those that will always doubt my change but that's okay, too. The only thing that really matters now is that Jesus knows and I know that I devoted my life to serving Him and saving lives for Him—here and now. Jesus took away my desire to do drugs and be sexually promiscuous. He took away the violence in me—I have not had a fight in over seven years!! That says a lot!

Jesus has given me a new zeal for educating myself (a very important necessity for life and self-confidence!), and I am now in college. After emotionally alienating my family for so many years due to my drug abuse, Jesus helped me tear down my walls and now my family and I are closer than we have ever been! My whole attitude toward life has changed. I am a new person in Jesus, and although the road has been hard, here I sit, at peace on death row. But believe me it would not be possible without Jesus Christ in my life!

Although this a very condensed biography I would be glad to answer any questions anyone may have. Just write and ask and I will be painfully honest in my answers, and in any advice I may have to anyone who may want it. Please realize the choices you make not only affect you, but they affect everyone around you. I pray God will guide all of you and touch your hearts.

In Jesus' Loving Name,

Karla
TX Death Row Inmate #777
Executed February 3, 1998

CHAPTER 8

David

*M*y name is David Ray and I'm on death row in Texas. My first encounter with police was at age thirteen. From that point forward I became well known to police as a troublesome kid and had the reputation of being "bad." This was something I desired in my youth—to be known as a tough guy was an honorable thing—I thought. The reason I wanted the bad reputation was because I didn't know anything else. I didn't know how to love and didn't know what it was to be loved. In short, I was confused, full of anger, hate, and spite.

Like many youths I turned to drugs and alcohol. These things made me part of the "in-crowd". I was cool and being cool was all part of the tough-guy image. In reality, the drugs and alcohol were only escape-mechanisms; they allowed me to escape from the reality of life . . . the reality of loneliness and the inability to cope with the everyday problems of my life. Yet, when sober and the "high" was gone, the problems loomed evermore on the horizon. I went through periods of trying to stay "high" all the time, but that didn't work because drugs and booze cost money—money a teenager simply doesn't have.

Since I needed money to provide my drugs and alcohol, I turned to crime as a means of obtaining money. I would steal anything I could sell. I committed my first armed robbery at 16 while on probation for burglary and stealing a motorcycle. At 16 I was a witness in the trial of a murdered police officer. The accused was convicted and sentenced to death. However, he was innocent of the charges and knew absolutely nothing about the officer's murder.

Having testified for the State at 16 I knew full well how the justice system was prone to operate. A sensible thing would have been to cease all criminal activity. I tried, but only in a superficial, half-hearted way.

I could take you through an entire life of crime, but I think it suffices to say, I became a career criminal. My criminal activity was closely related to the use of drugs and alcohol. Even when I had plenty of money and could buy drugs and alcohol, I would still go out and commit crimes. I became addicted to the element of danger involved in crime, the element of being caught, and the element danger of escape—if that became necessary.

After serving over five years in California's prison system, I came back to Texas. Like many people, I vowed never to return to prison. Only nine months later, I found myself in police custody charged with capital murder. It was a senseless thing, like most murders are. There I was facing another stretch in prison, except this time the authorities wanted to exterminate me. Just like you put an unwanted dog to sleep—the State contended I was just like that dog—unwanted and without purpose. This was hard for me to believe or accept.

While in the Beaumont City Jail one of the jailers began witnessing to me about Jesus Christ. I was skeptical and asked, "Why does God cause so many people to suffer, and why does He cause death and destruction? Why would such a merciful and loving God allow such things?" His answer was one that I didn't expect. He told me, "God *doesn't cause tragedies, death, or destruction. Satan causes all those things. God only allows them to happen." I'd never heard this before and thought his answer was curious, and my interest in his words grew. The jailer gave me a Bible to read in my cell. I read the chapters and verses he had referred me to.*

As I read, my heart grew heavy with sorrow about all the sin in my life. I desperately needed God's forgiveness; I knew in my heart Jesus Christ could give me peace and happiness in my life. I asked Jesus Christ to come into my heart and asked His forgiveness for my sins. After I had prayed the sinner's prayer and wept for some time, I felt a great burden had been lifted from me. I knew Jesus Christ had forgiven me of my sins and taken the burden away.

Being a Christian in prison isn't the easiest thing in the world. So, I strongly recommend you make a decision to serve God now rather than later. In prison, if you're a Christian, many of your fellow prisoners will think you're weak or scared, and hiding behind Christianity. However, I think the opposite is true—only the strong can live a life for Christ inside prison. However, it's not of themselves, it's only through the strength Jesus gives that we are able to live for Him in here.

Unlike the criminal justice system, God doesn't make deals. He wants us to serve Him one hundred percent or not at all. He will allow you to make the choice of serving Him or serving Satan; but He also wants you to know serving Satan has a price, not only in this life, but in the next life, too. As long as you are not serving God it's highly unlikely He will intercede in your life and bless you. Sure you might prosper serving Satan, but your prosperity is translated into eternal damnation. So, perhaps the choice you have to make is 'temporary prosperity' in this life, or 'eternal life' with Jesus Christ. I know of no greater riches than eternal life with Christ.

Even being on death row, Jesus has a plan for my life. So you can rest assured He has a plan for your life, too. I hope and pray you will make wise choices in your life and not end up here where I am, or in another part of the prison system.

In Jesus Christ's Name, Sincerely yours,

Dave
TX Death Row #827
Executed June 30, 2004

CHAPTER 9

Alvin

*M*y *name is Alvin and I am presently on Death Row in Livingston, Texas. I am writing this in an effort to reach young adults. If you are reading this, chances are, I am writing to you. I hope to open your eyes and enlighten you about how easy it is to make wrong choices.*

I grew up in the small country town of Quitman, Texas and had a fairly normal childhood. My father was a mechanic and my mother, a housewife and homemaker. I went to church and was baptized at the age of 13, but I never had a personal relationship with Jesus Christ. I only attended church because all the other kids were going and I wanted to fit in.

I did my share of partying and drinking while growing up and was pretty wild; however, I had never used drugs. In 1968, at the age of 17, I joined the United States Marine Corps. I served my time in the service and was honorably discharged in 1970. By this time I was well trained in self-discipline and had a good idea of what I wanted out of life. I started working in the oil fields for a couple of years and then moved to Longview, Texas. There I worked at Goodyear Tires. Finally, I moved to Tyler, Texas and opened my own business in 1981, a 24-hour diesel truck shop. It was then that I was first introduced to drugs, specifically methamphetamine, more commonly known as "crystal meth." I thought this drug would help me keep up the long hours that were required to operate the business. **Was I ever wrong!**

Having what I thought was considerable self-discipline, which I was taught in the Marine Corps, I thought I had everything under control. However, I was not prepared for the effect this drug would have upon me. Like so many others, I thought I could stop any time I wanted. Unfortunately, I was wrong again! The <u>only sure way to stop a drug habit is to never start</u>. The drugs took over my life. Drugs controlled everything I did and drugs were all I lived for.

The diesel truck shop was a booming and successful business. I had several family members working for a hired hand and I. After a year or so it got to the point where I was more concerned with getting some more dope than whether the business was running smoothly. I eventually left the shop to my younger brother Ricky while I ran the streets looking for dope. As time passed I became so addicted that drugs were my only concern. Nothing else and no one else mattered. The business began to crumble and I blamed everyone but myself. They finally had enough of me and left—wanting nothing to do with me. This left me to run the shop on my own. As a result of my drug addiction, I lost everything I had worked for <u>including my family</u>.

I have two daughters and two sons. Due to my drug use and never ending pursuit of drugs, I was not the loving and concerned father to them that they needed and deserved. They were shuttled back and forth between their mother and me, if and when I was ever around. I failed them and eventually lost them, too.

At the age of 36, I found myself in jail facing drug charges and nothing left to live for—or so I thought. All my "friends" in the drug world had washed their hands of me since I was of no use to them in jail. Sitting in my cell, I began to look back over all I had done and asked myself, "Why? Why had I destroyed everything I had worked for? Why had I alienated the very people I loved?" The answer: "Drugs!"

I had gotten into trouble and was placed in a single cell, maximum security. I was held there for nine months awaiting trial. There was no television or radio and all I was allowed to have was a Bible. So I started reading it. At first it was out of sheer boredom, but the more I read, the more interesting it became. I read all about Noah, Abraham, Moses and so on. After a while I became aware of a change—I really was interested in what I was reading and I felt a peacefulness in my heart for the first time in ten years. I really took a long, hard look at the past ten years of my life. I prayed, asking God to give me understanding of what I was reading. I didn't ask Him for freedom or for help. I only asked for TRUE understanding of His Word.

As time passed and I continued to read and study the Word, God opened my eyes to the answer to ALL my troubles: Jesus Christ. <u>So in 1987, right there in that maximum security cell I asked Jesus to come into my life.</u> I had succeeded in making a total mess of my life; I turned my life over to Christ so He could work His will. After turning my life over to Jesus, I asked to be baptized and the volunteer chaplain made all the arrangements. When I was baptized I experienced the presence of God in my life and the new birth my baptism symbolized. As I praised God and prayed while others were being baptized, I could tell there was a change in my life.

By a miracle, I was allowed to return to the general population. I praised God for this miracle because it gave me the opportunity to share what Jesus Christ had done in my life. I have stood with Jesus Christ ever since that day. Even through all of my legal trials I have never taken my eyes off Christ. I know that God has a plan for everything as long as I let His will be done in my life and give Him the glory.

Jesus died for me at Calvary and I intend to live for Him here on death row, or wherever God may take me. Through the love of the precious Savior, Jesus Christ, I have been reunited with my children again. In 1990, I was returned to the county jail and charged with capital murder in a murder that happened in 1984. I still clung to my faith in the Lord because I know that Jesus Christ is real in my life. I have full confidence the Lord is still in control of my life.

Another thing I want you to know is that I am innocent of the crime for which I am here on death row. However, because of my association and reputation in the drug world, the courts were able to convict me unjustly . . . Not because I am guilty, but because I made the wrong "choice" long ago to use drugs and run in the wrong crowd. I thought I was a big man then, and everyone was afraid of me. I thought they respected me. I was so caught up in my own world (of drugs) that I didn't think or care about what could happen in the future. So, you see, who you run with and what you choose to do with your time will play a very important part in how your life turns out. I'm here on death row because I made wrong choices and alienated everyone who might care. You don't have to kill someone to end up on death row; you can get here by just hanging with the wrong crowd.

You now have the chance to make good choices in your life. A lot of people think it's "cool" to do drugs, but I can tell you, there are a lot of "cool dudes" on death row. So, make your choices wisely. Stay away from drugs, and ask Jesus Christ into your life. You can make the right choice in your life, and I assure you, a choice to serve Jesus Christ is a choice you won't ever regret. He is the answer to all problems. You make the choice.

Alvin
TX Death Row Inmate #999012
Executed October 14, 2008

CHAPTER 10

Attention! Attention! Attention!

Now that I have your attention, I greet you in the name of my Lord and Savior, Jesus Christ. Father God, I pray in the name of Jesus, that your Holy Spirit will arrest the attention and minister to everyone that reads this testimony. In Jesus' Name! Amen!

I am a 33 year old Louisiana Death Row Inmate. I have been incarcerated since August 15, 1995. I arrived here on Death Row on September 5, 1997.

Please do not feel sorry for me. Being sent to Death Row was the best thing that could have happened to me, considering the lifestyle I once lived, even though I am innocent of this charge. This letter is not about my present situation. How many of you know . . . "What man meant for evil against me, God meant for my good!" The Bible states, "For we know that all things work together for good to them that love God, to them who are called according to his purpose."(Romans 8:28).

Last year, on October 28, 2002, early on Monday morning, I was leading our church service (here on Death Row) in praise and worship. While singing, I was overwhelmed by the power of the Holy Spirit! I started crying and speaking in a new language! To attempt to put words together to express the way I felt or what I felt would be an understatement.

I thought I knew God because my mother raised me in church (Church of God in Christ). But last year I realized that up until now, I knew about God; I did not know God. I have seen the movement of the Holy Spirit many times in and out of church. I truly believe in the power of the Holy Spirit. I can remember the Holy Spirit trying to come over me a couple of times. Once when I was sixteen years old, I was in the Louisiana Training Institute (L.T.I.) for boys in Bridge City, Louisiana. I had formed a little singing group. One night in 1986, the guard had my little singing group in the sleeping area practicing songs. I was leading the song, "Fill My Face with Tears", I felt the Holy Spirit trying to cover me. Out of pride and ignorance, I quenched the Spirit. I did not surrender to it. A couple of years later, I was in Monroe, Louisiana (L.T.I.) after being transferred from Bridge City. I put together another gospel singing group. While practicing there, I experienced the same thing again, and again I quenched the Spirit.

I had a "Jonah Spirit." I was running, trying to run from God. How many of you know that you cannot run from God!?! God is omnipresent! God is everywhere at the same time! He (God) is also Omniscient—He is all-knowing! He knew exactly what it would take to make me humble myself and surrender my life to Him—and say "Yes!" to His will for me. Many people have told me that I was a nothing but a loser. I thank God, that He is omnipotent (all powerful). He specializes in taking nothings and making somethings! He takes losers and makes not just winners but champions! Hallelujah! Amen!

I was water-baptized on October 9, 2003, almost a full year after I received the baptism of the Holy Spirit. I started a seven-day fast the same day (seven days without food!) I was seeking God's purpose and telling Him I will do whatever He wants me to do. He told me in order for Him to use me, I needed to be free. No! I am not talking about physical freedom right now. I am talking about spiritual and mental freedom. I inquired about what God meant. Then, He answered me, "The enemy, Satan is holding you in bondage." I am thinking, "How this could be!" He said, "All those little dark secrets you are afraid to tell anybody about and the things you have participated in that you are embarrassed about, I (God) want you to tell everybody about all that stuff." I thought to myself, what would people say!?! Or, how would they see me? They would think I am a monster! Then I realized, "I am a new creature in Christ Jesus! Old things are passed away. Behold! All things are become new." (2 Cor. 5:17).

Then, I think, "I am crucified with Christ; nevertheless I live, yet not I, but Christ within me. And the life which I now live in flesh, I live by the faith of the Son of God, who love me, and gave himself for me" (Galatians 2:20). Okay God, yes! Now I understand; it is not about me; It is all about Who is living in me! Now it is all about Jesus!!

Allow me to share this illustration with you . . . Say you were running for office to be the next president and you have a very good chance of winning the White House. Then you receive a call and the persons tell you, "Do you remember when you did this or that? If you don't give me a million dollars or your darkest secrets are going to be published." Now, you are afraid of being exposed and messing up your opportunity to become president. You allow the caller to manipulate you and you give in to all the caller's commands. Think about that!?! The caller has power over you because you fear what the information would do to your reputation. He can blackmail you forever, if you allow him to do so. So he has you in mental bondage.

But what if the caller said, "If you don't give me a million dollars, I am going to go public with this information." However, when he hangs up, you call and set up a press conference and go public with the information, yourself. What you actually did was take back the power from the blackmailer, right? So he can no longer hold you in bondage!!!

Check this out, now! You are standing before a large crowd of people in church giving your testimony or preaching the Word. Something catches your attention out of the corner of your eye. When you turn to look, you see Sister Ellis leaning over telling Deacon Jones something. Sister Ellis knows all about your little secrets. So, when you see her whispering to Deacon Jones, the Devil starts all kinds of thoughts in your mind. Sister Ellis only told Deacon Jones she is cooking dinner for her and his families. Satan is telling you that she is telling all your business. You lose focus and start trying to justify what you think she is saying about you. But, on the other hand, if you just empty yourself completely of all those little dark secrets, when you see someone you know whispering while you are preaching or testifying, they can only be bearing witness to what you are saying if they are even talking about you! Amen!!!

By emptying yourself, Satan cannot use your past sins and secrets to attack you with fear or hinder you from being available for God to work through you. Now, you are mentally free and the Holy Spirit can work His Will in your life, delivery you from bondage, taking out that old stony heart, and giving you a heart of flesh so He can place His Spirit in it. The Bible states, "If we confess our sins, he is faithful and just to forgive us our sins and to cleanse us from all unrighteousness" (1 John 1:9).

Once I got the revelation of that, all I could do is cry. The Bible states: "If the Son therefore shall make you free, ye shall be free indeed" (John 8:36).

And today, I sit here in bondage, physically, but spiritually and mentally, I am free! God showed me I am going to have an outreach ministry to win souls for His Kingdom. I am thinking: Lord, I can't preach but he told me: "Bobby, your testimony is your ministry!" The Bible states: "And they overcame him by the blood of the Lamb and by the word of their testimony and they loved not their lives unto death" *(Revelation 12:11).*

I know many people are saying that we have a jailhouse religion. But, I don't allow what they say to get to me, because I don't have religion; I have Jesus with the Holy Spirit working in and through me! One "freeman" (guard) told me he looks down on all prisoners. I explained to him that Jesus was a prisoner, too!!!

Many volunteer chaplains and ministers come in here to comfort us and to show they love and care about our soul. But, when they visit us, they end up getting blessed and encouraged through our testimonies. There are real men of God in this prison!!!

If you are interested in hearing more of my testimonies, I would love to share them with you. And, if any of you would like to share testimonies with me, I would love to hear them. If any of you are interested in joining me in a 24-hour fast beginning February 7, 2004, please write me for more information concerning the fast and feel free to send any requests you wish for us to stand in agreement with you about.

The Word of God states, *"Again I say unto you, that if two of you shall agree on Earth as touching anything that they shall ask, it shall be done for them of my Father which is in heaven. For where two or three are gathered together in my name, there am I in the midst of them" (Matthew 18:19-20).*

Personally speaking, I do not claim to be a member of any particular denomination. I am convinced that is a door Satan uses to enter through and cause division inside the Body of Christ. Jesus stated in the Bible: *"Every kingdom divided against itself is brought to desolation; and every city or house divided against itself shall not stand" (Matthew 12:25).*

I am a "Christ-Follower." I am striving each and every day to be more Christ-like.

Well, I pray my testimony has been a help to someone. If so, please feel free to correspond with me at the address below.

Your Humble Brother and Servant in Christ,
Anonymous Death Row Inmate
Angola, Louisiana
Executed: date unknown

CHAPTER 11

Best Moment of my Life

*I*t is 7:02 a.m. September 4, 2009. Under normal circumstances, one would be extremely exhausted due to possibly only two hours of rest last night/this morning. But at about 11:00 pm last night, I was thinking what Jesus said when the disciples asked him what was the most important of God's commandments, and Jesus replies, "Love the Lord with all your Heart, with all your Soul, and with all your mind."

At this thought, I turned on my worship music and finally submitted myself fully to the Lord. I prayed heavily while listening to deep worship music. I held my hand high reaching up accepting Him and asking Him to fill me with his Holy Spirit, to wash all my impurities away, to take away any urge that may come over me, and to direct my path the way He wills and not of my own. I truly worshipped the Lord and told Him He is the number one in my life; No girl or possession, drugs or alcohol will ever come between me and Him; and I apologized for living in the ways of the world, just acknowledged His names, and poured out my Love for Him as I worshipped Him more than I ever have before. I was completely honest and sincere and believed in Him without any disbelief.

Unexpectedly, this steady light tingling started in my fingertips held up high as I reached out and longed for His presence. As I continued to pray and worship, the little tingling in my fingertips remained, but it quickly began at the tips of my toes while lying in bed and within five seconds it grew so fast and strong that it felt like an out-of-this-world strong intense tingling glow. It was a sensation of several feelings combined. I can only attempt to explain this feeling to you but nothing I can say would be enough to measure the amount of Good that surged through my body. It was almost like a lightning bolt, but that still couldn't hold a candle to how incredible and strong this experience felt. I could describe it as Supernatural Power and the highest level of Love one could only try to imagine. The glowing surge also could be described as a healing feeling; if I had been deaf, blind, or sick in any way, I have no doubt that I would have been instantly healed in that amazing five seconds. It strongly conveyed "LIFE" and Purpose and the Power of Creation. It made me think of the Creation of Adam.

I know without a shadow of a doubt, God filled me with His Holy Spirit last night, and that feeling of flawless perfection was almost too much power and pure good to allow me to feel in my imperfect human body. After this I began to cry with the happiest tears a man could ever cry. I spoke, "Lord, I'm not worthy" three times while I continued to cry. Later, I realized I said that because I was more aware of my sins from the moment He allowed me to feel his perfect Holy Spirit. I was amazed that he would die on the cross for a sinner like me.

After I collected my tears, I continued to worship leading myself out of the bed and onto my knees on the wood floor. While transitioning from the bed to the floor, directly after the warmth of his eternal embrace of Love, I noticed I had very little energy and staggered when trying to arise as my legs were weak and my arms as well. I was on my way to the floor anyway to worship the One and Only King of Kings and Lord of Lords. I tell you the truth, I am not 99.9 percent sure that this was God; I am 110 percent certain that God's presence overflowed my body in just the short time of my experience. It was better than any feeling the world would have to offer! My sins made me feel truly not worthy to feel such good. It reminded me of all the people just wanting to touch Jesus' cloak in the Bible.

My philosophy teacher has really been trying to destroy and question my Christian faith as well as the faith of everyone else in the class; but regardless, it just made me more and more interested in finding my Lord and studying Biblical History. Although the professor speaks with confidence and puts his energy in questioning the unknown, he runs circles in your head and confuses you. This is how it was at first for me in that class. Just the thought of no God, no purpose and things just happen and we die and are no more, was extremely disturbing and caused me some depression for the first couple of days, but it inspired me to research the historical and archeological sources of the Christian faith. I am truly grateful for that inspiration, because I believed in God even in the darkness and now He has truly blessed me with a taste of the highest happiness beyond the limits of this world that one could ever hope to achieve, to say the least!

This is my experience at the age of 20 years old and I confirm that these words are in every way true and not a thread of fiction is incorporated in this writing. I will never again think of doubting God. There is no way a philosophy teacher or wise man on earth could now tell me there is no God.

1st Corinthians 2:4—"My message and preaching were not with wise and persuasive words but with demonstrations of the Spirit Power so that your faith might not rest on man's wisdom but on God's Power."

Anonymous youth on probation
Guided by Bill to avoid Prison

CHAPTER 12

Revelation Dream

I just woke up with a crazy dream on my mind and when the meaning hit me, it was so monumentally amazing. This was one of those few dreams where you know it came straight from Papa!

It started out in some big field that was really green with clover patches and various canals throughout the field. The way it appeared was surreal, like a fairy tale setting almost with bright light conditions and further analysis of it now, reminds me of a field trip where people were roaming around almost like you do with your families while visiting the zoo. It seemed like Baylor was behind us at the opposite end of the field in which we were heading. I was alone for the first part of the dream. Everyone in the dream wandering around was slowly making their way towards the main attraction, but I like to go straight to the point. I was on my way to this main attraction that everyone somehow knew of beforehand. It apparently was so amazing for some reason, almost like it had been advertised or rather rumors had reached everyone by spreading the word regarding this new discovery, invention, or creation.

As I approached this final canal, it was covered with clovers and bright green foliage everywhere, waist-deep with ripples and gentle waves of green grass and clovers overflowing the canal where the couple of people in the dream and I had to walk through a swamp area to get to the final destination where this red barn was. People were standing at a round stage inside the barn. As I approached the barn, while currently standing in waist-deep water with a layer of grass and clover on top of it, I could hear people whispering. It was like you were at the zoo and was excited to see your favorite animal and it's not there. I continued toward the barn because I was eager to get to the stage and be able to make out the faint echoes from the announcer (he sounded like an auctioneer) on the stage. I got inside the barn as the announcer was describing this new thing created. Everyone marveled as he went on to explain his amazing creation, saying it was new to science and a new discovery of life. He went on to say, in an astonished and mystical voice, that it had a free will. This exclamation made everyone in the crowd sigh in awe of such a wonder. It took the form of a little grasshopper/moth that was flying around just out of reach where everyone was looking up at it fly around. It couldn't fly very far for long periods of time and as a result, when it got closer to me, it landed on my arm. This is when part one ends and part two begins.

Part two of the dream takes the setting of the old neighborhood I used to live in. My youngest brother was playing around on the sidewalk and it seemed like we were in front of one of his friend's house. I looked on my arm and there was the grasshopper still. I was overjoyed like I was taking good care of it and this brought me joy.

It then began to fly away and wander around, so I patiently was chasing it to and fro all over the place waiting for it to get tired and land. The further it was away from me, the sadder I became. It landed on a bush. Just about the time it was flying towards me it kept flying just out of my reach, past me, and landed in the street flopping around frantically trying to get back upright to take off again. As usual, I was worried and rushed to its aid in fear it may get run over on the busy street. I fixed *it in the right position on my hand and as much as I wanted to keep it on my hand where it was safe, I let it take off slowly, knowing that it would need me to remain close with my eye on it in the event it would desperately, yet unknowingly, require my intervention again.*

The revelation that I received through this dream was like a freight train when it hit me a little while ago. I have yet to interpret what everything in the dream means, but I do know that the main purpose for it was that God was letting me see how much He really loves and cares about us by allowing me to experience that analogy. He showed me through this dream how extremely faithful He is to us and how He always remains by our side even though we are oblivious to His presence most of the time. Also the dream revealed to me that despite God's many efforts, our free-will makes us hard to hold on to; we often make Him chase us around, which He does passionately, because He is full of hope for us that we may turn to Him and land on His arm where we will be safe and not grow weary. He truly is a good God and He desires to teach us with His wisdom and help us develop into something grand if we will just stay close and walk in God's ways.

Same Anonymous Youth on probation
Guided by Bill to avoid Prison

CHAPTER 13

End-Time Scripture Considerations

According to Bible, in the end times, expect widespread deception, counterfeit miracles, and the appearance of false prophets. Each of these evils will contribute to an atmosphere that will deceive an untold number of people throughout the world. The Antichrist, possibly a charismatic Muslim with a fake Jesus as a sidekick, will convince his followers that he is the answer to the world's problems. Paul tells us that those who become caught in the antichrist's web of deceit will be guilty because they freely choose to enjoy evil while denying the truth.

END TIME SIGNS

1. **False Bible teachers are money hungry.** They would be smooth talkers, have many followers, and slur the Christian faith (2 Peter 2:1-3)

2. **Homosexuality is increasingly evident** at the end of the Age. (2Timothy 3:3)

3. **Earthquakes** are in diverse places. (Matthew 24:7)

4. **Stress is** a part of everyday living. (2 Timothy 3:1)

5. **Many wars** erupt. (Matthew 24:6)

6. People **forsake the Ten Commandments** as a moral code, committing adultery, stealing, lying, and killing. (Matthew 24:12)

7. There is a **cold religious system, in denying God's power.** (2 Timothy 3:5)

8. Men **substitute fantasy in place of Christian truth.** (2 Timothy 4:4) This is so evident at Christmas

9. **Deadly diseases are prevalent.** (Matthew 24:7) The worldwide increase in AIDS deaths is almost inestimable. Over 160,000 Americans die of cancer each year.

10. The **fact that God once flooded the earth** (Noah's flood) **is denied.** (2 Peter 3:5-6)

11. **The institution of marriage is forsaken** by many. (1 Timothy 4:3)

12. There is an **increase in famines.** (Matthew 4:7)

13. **Vegetarianism is increasing**. (1 Timothy 4:3-4)

14. There is a **cry for peace.** (1 Thessalonians 5:3)

15. **The possession of Jerusalem is at the center of international turmoil.** (Zechariah 12:3).

16. **Knowledge is increasing.** (Daniel 12:4)

17. **There are hypocrites within the Church**. (Matthew 13:25-30)

18. There is an **increase of religious cults/false teachers**. (Matthew 24:11 & 24)

19. The future seems fearful to many. (Luke 21:26)

20. Humanity is becoming materialistic. (2 Timothy 3:4)

21. Many are involved in travel. (Daniel 12:4)

22. The **Christian Gospel is being preached** as a warning **to all nations.** (Matthew 24:14)

23. Jesus said **Christians are hated** "for His name's sake." (Matthew 24:9)

24. And there are signs in the sun, and in the moon, and in the stars; and upon the earth distress of nations, with perplexity; the sea and the waves roaring; Men's hearts are failing them for fear, and for looking after those things which are coming on the earth: for the powers of heaven are shaken. (Luke 21:25-26)

25. **Youth are rebellious**. For men are lovers of their own selves, covetous, boasters, proud, blasphemers, disobedient to parents, unthankful, unholy. (2 Timothy 3:2)

26. **Men mock the warning signs of the end of the age** saying, "For since the fathers fell asleep, all things continue as they were from the beginning of the creation." (2 Peter 3:4) The Bible even reveals their motivation; they love lust (verse 3). They fail to understand that a day to the Lord is as a thousand years to us. God is not subject to the time that He created. He can flick through time as we flick through the pages of a history book. The reason He seems to be silent, is because He is patiently waiting, not willing that any perish, but that all come to repentance.

Compiled by
Anonymous youth on probation
Guided by Bill to avoid Prison

CHAPTER 14

Inspirational Poems by Matthew Chance

Expectations

Expectations are faith in future sought,
In Yours or others, if fulfilled or not.

Fortunes were never meant to be shown,
Fate takes course no matter if known

Some rely on the actions of the rest,
Contents of tomorrow they try to guess.

Choice is the only power we've been gifted,
From expectations future remains unshifted.

Foresight is enclosed with an unbreakable seal,
Our choice is all that can affect what our future reveals.

Before it is heard, s song is written note by note.
AS so in life, choice by choice, we compose.

If good is anticipated, surprise is deferred.
If the prediction is faulty, disappointment occurs.

What is to come cannot be told,
Decisively we potters of life will mold.

The wisest of ways is to never expect,
But through choice attain desired effect.

Purpose

Purpose is an elusive truth,
Sought out by many,
Ignored at youth.

There is a reason for creation,
Rarely do we find,
And can be lost for the duration
Of a full lifetime.

Stay true to yourself and know what is right,
And it will soon be revealed,
Have a goal and never lose sight,
Your life you'll learn to wield.

CHAPTER 15

Prison Chaplain Interview by William Ramsey

A young man who is 29 years old came to speak with me about his problem with alcoholism. He has recently been born again and is finding it very difficult to give all things to God and trust only in Him. He has struggled with his alcoholism for 15 years, has never been married, and works in the retail industry. He is a friend from church who feels he can relate to me because I've overcome, with God's help, the same issues he is looking to overcome.

Coding: CH: Chaplain Bill DG: Person being interviewed

CH: *What can I help you with?*

DG: *Well, as you know, I've had an ongoing problem with alcoholism for the past 15 years and am finding it very hard to trust in God and overcome my constant struggle with drinking.*

CH: *Well, you take it one day at a time. I have a little prayer that I say every morning when I get up. "Lord, help me today to do your will and not my will. Help me today to not take a drink, not want a drink, or not need a drink. In Jesus' name, Amen"*

DG: How can that really help me? It doesn't seem like just saying a prayer will help my constant struggles because they seem so big.

CH: Well, it does if you do it by faith. *"Faith comes by hearing and hearing by the word of God."* In other words, you have to read the Bible daily and follow God's promises and practice them daily. I want you to read Phil 4:13 every morning and stand on the promise that you can do all things through Christ which includes not taking that first drink.

DG: Thank you, Bill. I will do that, and I'll see you next week.

EVALUATION:

Client:

DG is struggling with alcoholism and finding his strength in God. I think he feels that his problem is too big for God to handle but is actively seeking Christian guidance. I plan to continue meeting with him on a weekly basis and encouraging him in the Lord.

Chaplain:

Having gone through the struggles of alcoholism myself, I can relate and understand what he is going through right now. I know the loneliness and pain that is felt when one is tumbling through the daily motions while falling to alcohol. I feel a need to help and guide him in accordance with the Bible. With trust in God, he will be able to deal with his problems.

Theological and Growth Concerns:

He needs to learn to lean on God to overcome problems that seem too big to overcome, and he needs to realize that God is bigger and stronger than he is, and if he puts all his trust in God he will be able to overcome anything.

Phil 4:13, "I can do all things through Christ
who strengthens me."
February 2, 2005

Connect with God

You have read the story of parts of my life and the testimonies of other prisoners who found Christ as their Savior while in prison or trying to avoid prison. Perhaps you find yourself in a similar jam like any of them. Christ is the Answer! Christ is the only Answer! He is the Author and Finisher of our faith (Romans 12:1-2). How about you connect with Jesus Christ right now? Let's pray . . .

Dear Jesus, I am a sinner. Forgive me all my sins. Save my soul. I repent all of my sins and ask you to come into my heart and be the Lord and Master of my life. Take control of my life. I give myself to you. Thank you for hearing my prayer and saving my soul. In Jesus' name I pray. Amen

WHAT NOW?

1. Confess Jesus Christ with your mouth and **be baptized.** Acts 2:41, Matthew 10:32, 28:19–20

2. **Join a churc**h where the **Bible is preached** and Jesus is Lord. Hebrews 10:25

3. **Pray daily**. I Thessalonians 5:17

4. **Read and meditate on the Word of God daily**. Acts 17:11

5. **Witness—Share Christ daily.** Acts 1:8

6. **Be filled with the Holy Spirit**. Ephesians 5:18

7. **Obey God's nudges**: do what God says to do.

Helpful Scriptures

(Citing NKJV: New King James Version)

Read all scriptures in context (read at least two verses before and two verses after). In addition to the preceding scriptures, read and heed the following:

Deuteronomy 28:1-14 *Diligently obey the voice of God and you will be blessed by God.*

Psalms 139:1-18 . . . *God knew you in your mother's womb* (verses 13, 16)

Proverbs 3:5-6 . . . *Trust in the LORD with all your heart, and lean not on your own understanding. In all yours ways acknowledge Him, and He will direct your paths.*

Proverbs 18:21 . . . *The tongue has the power of life and death, and those who love it will eat its fruit.*

Jeremiah 29:11 . . . *For I know the thoughts that I think toward you, says the LORD, thoughts of peace and not of evil, to give you a future and a hope.*

John 3:16 . . . *God so loved the world, He gave His only begotten Son, that whosoever believes on Him will have everlasting life.*

John 11:35 . . . *Jesus wept. (See also Matthew 26:75 & Mark 14:72.)*

John 14:6 ... *Jesus said, "I am the way, the truth, and the life. No man comes to the Father but by me."*

John 14:21 ... *He who has My commandments and keeps them, it is he who loves Me. And he who loves Me will be loved by My Father, and I will love him and manifest Myself to him.*

John 15:5 ... *I am the vine, you are the branches. He who abides in me, and I in him, bears much fruit; for without Me you can do nothing.*

Romans 3:23 ... *For all have sinned and come short of the glory of God*

Romans 6:23 ... *The wages of sin is death, but the gift of God is eternal life through Jesus Christ our Lord.*

1 Corinthians 10:13 ... *There has no temptation taken you but such as is common to man; God is faithful; He will not tempt you above you are able but He will make a way of escape that you can bear it.*

2 Corinthians 5:17 ... *Therefore if any man in Christ, he is a new creation; old things have passed away; behold, all things have become new.*

1 John 4:4 ... *You are of God, little children, and have overcome them, because He who is in you is greater than he who is in the world.*

Ephesians 6:10-18 ... *Be strong in the Lord and in the power of His might. Put on full armor of God that you may be able to stand against the wiles of the devil* ... withstand in the evil day, *and having done all, to stand* ... *belt of truth, breastplate of righteousness, shoes of preparation of peace, shield of faith, helmet of salvation, sword of the Spirit (Word of God)* ...

Philippians 4:6-7 ... *Be anxious for nothing ... prayer & supplication, let your requests be made known to God* ... *peace of God will guard your hearts and minds in Christ Jesus.*

Philippians 4:13 . . . *I can do all things through Christ who strengthens me.*

Philippians 4:19 . . . *My God shall supply all your needs according to His riches in Christ Jesus.*

James 1:5 . . . *If you lack wisdom, ask of God who gives to all liberally.*

Read at least two verses before and after, considering all the above scriptures plus the following:

Colossians 3:20 . . . *Children, obey your parents in all things for this is well pleasing to the Lord.* God's Word rules supreme: obey when it is in line with God's Word.

Matthew 18:19-20 . . . *Again I say to you that if two of you agree on earth concerning anything that they ask, it will be done for them by my Father in heaven. For where two or three are gathered together in my name, I am in the midst of them.*

Luke 21:28 . . . *Look up and lift up your heads, because your redemption draws near.*

James 4:17 . . . *To him who knows to do good and does not do it, to him it is sin.*

Helpful Resources

Especially for those Imprisoned:

Get an easy-to-read Bible or two.

Attend and participate in Chapel regularly.

Talk to chaplains, pastors, or priests. Be real.

Go to education classes to gain better knowledge and understanding as well as develop a trade. Do your very best to become all God has created you to become to fulfill your destiny (God's purpose for your life).

For those trying to turn your life around:

Get an easy-to-read Bible or two (different versions, and preferably one a study Bible).

Attend and participate in Church regularly. Get into a smaller home group or

Talk to pastors or priests. Be real.

Go to education classes to gain better knowledge and understanding as well as develop a trade. Do your very best to become all God has created you to become to fulfill your destiny (God's purpose for your life).

POSTSCRIPT

Authors' Afterthoughts

William Ramsey

The inhumane prison event portrayed in this book took place in the 1960's. Thank God, conditions have greatly improved in our current prison systems. Yet, each of the inmates incarcerated in today's system because of their bad choices are still deprived of their freedom and preferred life-style. Each is a soul to be rescued and saved.

I would like to say, now I have learned to forgive and even to pray for all those who hurt me, even as I pray that those I have hurt or caused pain, can forgive me. I understand I cannot receive forgiveness unless I give forgiveness. I must bless those who curse me and always return good for evil, because what we give out comes back to us in many ways.

I also wish to say I love my parents and I am praying for my family that they will find the blessings of God as I have found. My parents no longer drink. The generational alcoholic curse is now broken. Praise God! I've forgiven my parents for their mistakes and I hope and pray my children have forgiven me for my mistakes.

I know God has forgiven me, and I know He will care for my family as I care for His. He is a loving God. He's my Heavenly Father who loved me into submission to do His will. Give Him Praise and Glory!!

What hurts me most is when someone who is a Christian in prison gets out and comes back! Low knowledge of the Word of God (Bible) >> low faith level >> slip and fall. You have to stay in the Word and practice it in your life to get out of prison and stay out! See Psalms 119:9-11, Proverbs 3:5-6, John 14:6, and John 14:21.

Jesus loves you and has a plan, a special destiny for your life (Jeremiah 29:11). Whether or not we walk and live out that plan is up to us. The choice is ours. Joshua 24:15 says, *"... choose you this day whom you will serve."* Deuteronomy 30:19 says, *" ... I have set before you life and death, blessing and cursing: therefore choose life ..."*

What is your choice today?

Some Additional Thoughts

By Bill and Denise

During our prison ministry, we wrote to and spoke with Charles Manson, Tommy Lyn Sells, and others—giving them the opportunity and choice to come to know Jesus. But one had already lost his mind and the other would/could not turn his will over to God. But Alvin Kelly and Dave Harris did accept Christ and many, many more did.

One sticks out in my mind at Angola State Prison in Louisiana. I was going through the prison and asked to go in the lock up where no one goes. There I found a man way in the back. He had seen no one but meals for years. He sat on the floor near bars as I did. We talked a long, long time. I spent all my time there that day. I gave him a ring that turns around and around. It was a ring on top of a ring and I told him that like Jesus lives, it goes on forever and ever. I said, *"As you turn this ring remember how long Jesus will love you!"* He wept. I wept. It was awesome. It was sad to leave. He looked so sad.

Sin takes you further than you want to go . . . keeps you longer than you want to stay . . . and costs you more than you want to pay! But Jesus said in John 10:10, He *"died that you might have abundant life."* Are you living abundant life? Or, are you a slave to Satan's addictions and actions of pornography, drugs, nicotine, or sugar and gluttony?

Jesus is your hope of becoming the person God is building you to be . . . your destiny. When you first became a believer, you did not lose all of the characteristics of the "old life" overnight/ instantly. Some bad habits and sins Jesus may have removed from your experience immediately, but the correction of many problems is a process that involves time and gradual change. Philippians 2:12 says, " . . . *work out your own salvation with fear and trembling.*"

At times it is tempting to be discouraged about what you think is a lack of progress and then to bog down in feelings of inadequacy or insecurity. *"If I could only be like so-and-so,"* you might sigh privately when you look at the life of a believer you admire.

Jesus wants you to understand that you are not responsible for making the changes inside. Being conformed to the likeness of Christ (Romans 8:29) is a job for Him, and trying to take correction into your own hands only results in frustration, failure, and a hazardous shift into a performance-based mindset. The Lord promises to fulfill His purpose in and for your life, and along the way He hones your character and gives you abilities to do His work. (Psalm 138:8; Philippians 2:13).

Jesus is your hope of giving God honor and glory in heaven. He not only provides all you need for life today, but He is right now preparing a place in heaven for you which surpasses your imagination. (John 14:2-3). The suffering you endure here will be replaced by the uninterrupted glory of seeing your Savior face-to-face and worshipping Him in fullness forever. Romans 8:18 says, *"For I consider that the sufferings of this present time are not worthy to be compared with the glory that is to be revealed in us."*

With Christ in you, you become a living, breathing example of the hope He offers. That is why the Lord wants you to approach your daily affairs with this attitude: *"But sanctify Christ as Lord in your hearts, always being ready to make a defense to everyone who asks you to give an account for the hope that is in you, yet with gentleness and reverence"* (1 Peter 3:15). Jesus' hope is sure, His presence is real, and you are a special appointed agent of His hope to those who still need Him as Savior.

How I Became a Prison Chaplain

I became a prison chaplain in 1993 seven months after staying in God's Word day and night and hiding His Word in my heart. Yet, after Chaplaincy training and later becoming a Licensed Ordained minister, when I went through those prison doors and heard the loud slam behind me, my heart jumped up in my chest; I felt I could not swallow or breathe for a moment. But then I remembered God's Word and knew what to do. I quoted His Word, *"I can do all things through Christ Who strengthens me."* (Philippians 4:13) Another I quoted from Deuteronomy 28, *"I am blessed going in and I am blessing going out. I am the Righteousness of the Lord Jesus Christ."* But I always felt more blessed going out than going in! LOL! Praise the Lord! Glory to God! This book contains only half of all the horrendous things that happened in prison; if I shared them all, the book would be too long.

Slowly it became easier to go in to work for the Lord in prison behind those clanging doors. I went into almost every prison in Texas and Angola for fifteen years.

Now I am focused on getting out this book so I can get it into more hands by more people to help keep them from making the same or similar wrong choices in life and ending up hurting others and themselves. But when you have made poor choices and lived that kind of life, you must stay close to a strong mentor and memorize God's Word. Memorize it. Speak it. Share it with others. Speak it over yourself . . . forgetting what lies behind and reaching forward to what lies ahead (Philippians 3) and what God's Word says is true.

Forget the word curses your parents spoke over you or you heard them speak over each other. Wipe it out by quoting God's Word. Respond to those thoughts with, *"But God's Word says . . . ."* Like *"I am a new creation in Christ Jesus."* (2 Corinthians 5:17) Put it under the blood. Let go of it. Shake it off your hands! Speak the truth in response to all those lies; God's Word is the truth! *"Greater is He that is within me than he that is in the world!"*

As soon as I went into prison as a Chaplain, an inmate yelled, *"Bugsy, is that you?"* I turned and there was an Bandito biker friend. He said, *What game are you running now?"* I replied, *"Jimmy, it's no game. It is Jesus, It is real."* He listened and for three nights he could not sleep, from shock. Until he got cancer a year later and called for me to come to the place they sent him to, he could not accept Jesus. But there in that hospital bed he did. I had prayed he would accept Christ as His Savior and he did. *"Ask and believe and you shall receive"* (sometimes years later).

God blessed me with another Harley and a church full of Godly friends to ride with. Now I ride with Christ! Amen! No addictions. Just blessed! It is not easy at first to turn a lifetime around, but you can do it. I did with Christ's help! And I have seen others do it with God's help, too.

You can do all things through Christ Who strengthens you. (Philippians 4:13.) God will supply all your needs according to His riches in Glory by Christ Jesus. (Philippians 4:19.)

Ask Jesus to come into your heart. Get into God's Word; read it, meditate in it, memorize it. And share it with others. Find a strong Christian mentor and start moving forward on your Christian walk. If I can do it, anyone can do it! God enables all of us, if and when we ask.

About the Authors

William & Denise Ramsey

Both Denise and Bill were born and raised in Southeast Texas. He attended Port Arthur Business College. Making some poor choices including stealing cars landed him in prison for two years; he got out but went back for a total of four years in prison.

Bill was not raised in a Christian home, accepted Jesus about age 42, but really got serious with God when he studied the Bible starting about age 49. Denise was raised in a church-attending home, accepted Jesus as her Savior at age 10, walked with Him all of her life, backslid for three years, but recommitted her life to Christ at age 37. She was closely mentored by two pastors, Dr. Steve Hays and George Palmer, who taught her God's Word and how to live and walk it out. They also taught her unconditional love. The new keys were 1) studying and memorizing the Word and 2) the unconditional love.

Bill became a certified volunteer Chaplain through the Texas Volunteer Chaplaincy Ministry in 1994. In 1999, Bill and Denise completed the Faith-Based Counselor Training Institute course to become Certified Restorative Therapists. Bill became a Licensed Minister of the Gospel of Jesus Christ through Kingsway Fellowship International (Des Moines Iowa) as of April 1, 2004. Denise mostly wrote letters, occasionally going into the men's prison. Both Ministered in prisons for about fifteen years since 1993.

Bill retired from Chaplaincy ministry after Hurricane Ike (2008). Currently God is transitioning him to a ministry for children to help them make good choices to prevent incarceration. He also spends much time ministering to those who need hope on the streets of Austin.

We felt led of the LORD Jesus Christ to publish a book to tell Bill's story as well as to share the stories of others whose lives have been changed by the love of God. The goal and desire in publishing this book is to help prevent individuals from making similar choices and traveling similar paths leading to imprisonment.

Some Questions to Ponder

Are you a child who has lived through much neglect and/or abuse (physical, mental, verbal, or sexual)?

Are you a teen who is making some poor choices about friends, sex, drugs, alcohol, gangs, and bullying?

Are you a young adult who is making some poor choices about friends, sex, drugs, alcohol, etc.?

Are you an older adult who has lived a longer life of poor choices that have led you down a path of pain, heartache, broken relationships, and possibly imprisonment?

If you can answer "Yes!" to any of these questions, then this book is for you!

Are you a pastor, a prison chaplain, or a Christian with a heart to redirect teens and young adults to choices that lead to abundant life, health, and prosperity rather than jail and prison life?

If "Yes!" then this book is also for you.

If these do not apply to you or someone you love, how about helping younger people get plugged in to Jesus, learn to make healthy choices, and live a Christ-centered life to glorify God?

This book is for pastors, teachers, counselors, parents, everyone living in this 21st Century with all of its challenges.

Reversing the Curse

1 Samuel 2–4 promises that God reverses circumstances, makes the poor rich, the infertile fertile. He brings those who are low to high places and makes those who are weak strong. The nobody is made into somebody through Him.

"He will guard the feet of his saints, but the wicked
will be silenced in darkness.
It is not by strength that one prevails; those who oppose
the Lord will be shattered.
He will thunder against them from heaven;
the Lord will judge the ends of the earth.
He will give strength to his king and exalt the horn
of his anointed."
—1 Samuel 2:9–10

"Not by might nor by power, but by my Spirit,'
says the LORD Almighty."
—Zechariah 4:6

When you are filled with the Spirit of the Lord, He can change any circumstance to your favor. Don't be led by anyone back into the old places you've come from. You lead. Do not follow. Be strong enough to say, "I don't go that way anymore", because if you walk that way at all you will loose the strength that God has given you. Getting away from God ends in painful circumstances. ALWAYS. If you do slip and fall, as soon as you realize your in sin, repent and begin speaking God's blessings over your life.

(See **Deuteronomy 28:1–14** also **Numbers 6:24–26**)
Meditate on this **DAILY!**